ALL THE GREAT BOOKS (abridged)

*Reed Martin &
Austin Tichenor*

*additional material by
Matthew Croke &
Michael Faulkner*

BROADWAY PLAY PUBLISHING INC
56 E 81st St., NY NY 10028-0202
212 772-8334 fax: 212 772-8358
BroadwayPlayPubl.com

ALL THE GREAT BOOKS (abridged)
© Copyright 2005 by Reed Martin & Austin Tichenor

First printing: September 2005
Second printing: December 2005
Third printing: June 2006
I S B N: 0-88145-263-7

Book design: Marie Donovan
Word processing: Microsoft Word
Typographic controls: Xerox Ventura Publisher 2.0 P E
Typeface: Palatino
Printed and bound in the U S A

ABOUT THE AUTHORS

Reed Martin is a Managing Partner of the Reduced Shakespeare Company, which he joined in 1989. He co-created and performed in the original stage productions of THE COMPLETE HISTORY OF AMERICA (abridged), THE BIBLE: THE COMPLETE WORD OF GOD (abridged), WESTERN CIVILIZATION: THE COMPLETE MUSICAL (abridged), ALL THE GREAT BOOKS (abridged), and COMPLETELY HOLLYWOOD (abridged)—and contributed additional material to THE COMPLETE WORKS OF WILLIAM SHAKESPEARE (ABRIDGED).

Reed has written for the B B C, National Public Radio, Britain's Channel Four, R T E Ireland, Public Radio International, *The Washington Post*, and *Vogue* magazine. With Austin Tichenor he wrote the quasi-religious memoir*The Greatest Story Ever Sold,* as well as the comic Shakespeare reference book*Reduced Shakespeare* which is published by Hyperion.

He has been seen on all the major television networks, and has performed in forty-six states and eleven foreign countries.

Prior to joining the Reduced Shakespeare Company, Reed spent two years as a clown and assistant ringmaster with Ringling Brothers' Barnum & Bailey Circus.

Reed has a BA in both Theater and Political Science from the University of California at Berkeley and an

M F A in Acting from the University of California at San Diego. He is also a graduate of both Ringling Brothers' Barnum & Bailey Clown College and the Bill Kinnamon School of Professional Umpire Training. He lives in Northern California with his wife and two sons.

Austin Tichenor is a Managing Partner of the Reduced Shakespeare Company, which he joined in 1992. He co-created and performed in the original stage productions of THE COMPLETE HISTORY OF AMERICA (abridged), THE BIBLE: THE COMPLETE WORD OF GOD (abridged), WESTERN CIVILIZATION: THE COMPLETE MUSICAL (abridged), ALL THE GREAT BOOKS (abridged), and COMPLETELY HOLLYWOOD (abridged); the original film *The Ring Reduced*; and the radio productions of *The Reduced Shakespeare Radio Show*, *The Reduced Shakespeare Company Christmas*, and (for N P R's *All Things Considered*) *The Reduced Shakespeare Round Table*. He also starred in the P B S film version of *The Complete Works of William Shakespeare (abridged)*.

Prior to joining the R S C, Austin was Associate Producing Director of the American Stage Festival in Milford, NH, where he created Early Stages, A S F's New Play Series, served as Literary Manager/ Dramaturg, wrote stage adaptations of *A Christmas Carol* and *Frankenstein*, and directed several productions a season. He also developed A S F's Young Company, for which he wrote over twenty original plays and musicals for young audiences.

With his partner Dee Ryan, Austin wrote and developed the animated project *Fowl Play* for Disney, as well as the screenplays *Birds of a Feather* and *All The Other Reindeer*. With Reed Martin, he wrote the comic memoir *The Greatest Story Ever Sold*. And he's guest starred on many hours of episodic television, including recurring roles on *Everwood, 24, Alias, The Practice, Mister Sterling, Ally McBeal*, and *Felicity*, in addition to several movies and national commercials.

Austin has a B A in History and Dramatic Art from U C Berkeley and an M F A in Directing from Boston University. He's a member of the Dramatists Guild and an alumnus of the B M I Musical Theater Workshop.

He lives in Los Angeles with his wife and two children.

SPECIAL THANKS

For their contributions to the development of the script, the authors wish to thank Jane Martin, Dee Ryan, Megan Loughney, Don Martin, Lisa Croke, Viola Voris, Rachel Hamilton, Russell Lees, Leila and Robert Gordon, Ezra Weiss and Peter & Aliza Murrieta of L A's Bang Improv Studio, Charles Towers and Merrimack Repertory Theatre, Ed Stern and Cincinnati Playhouse in the Park, Geoff Alm, Steve Smith, Guillermo Gonzalez, Kent Thompson & Alan Harrison and Alabama Shakespeare Festival, Kea Watson, Andrea Atkins, Robin Selinger, and the audiences who came and laughed (or didn't) at the early workshops. Very special thanks to Matt and Mike, who made this thing come alive in rehearsal by finding the funny (and often adding it).

ALL THE GREAT BOOKS (abridged) was originally produced and performed by the Reduced Shakespeare Company. The first public performance was at bang. Improv Studio in Hollywood, CA on 24 January 2002 with the following cast:

COACH ....Reed Martin
PROFESSOR .... Austin Tichenor
STUDENT TEACHER .... Michael Faulkner

The show was subsequently performed at Merrimack Repertory Theater in Lowell, MA in March 2002, at Cincinnati Playhouse in the Park in July 2002, and at Alabama Shakespeare Festival in August 2002 with the following cast:

COACH .... Reed Martin
PROFESSOR .... Michael Faulkner
STUDENT TEACHER .... Matthew Croke

The show then opened at the Kennedy Center in
Washington, DC on June 12, 2003 with the cast:

COACH ....Reed Martin
PROFESSOR .... Austin Tichenor
STUDENT TEACHER ....Matthew Croke

Directors ....Reed Martin & Austin Tichenor
General Manager .... Megan Loughney
Technical Director .... Kea Watson
Fight Director ....Geoffrey Alm
Creative Consultant .... Steve Smith
Scenic Design .... Robertson Wellen
Props .... Erika Lilienthal, Shannon Rae Lutz,
                    Jenni Schwaner, Kea Watson
Costumes ...Erika Lilienthal, Frances Nelson McSherry,
                    Jenni Schwaner, Allison Stubbs
Dickensian Organ Riffs ....Charlie Christmas
Additional Voice .... Jane Martin

IMPORTANT NOTE

The name "Reduced Shakespeare Company®"
is a Registered Trademark, and its use in any way
whatsoever to publicize, promote, or advertise any
performance of this script is EXPRESSLY PROHIBITED.

Likewise, any use of the name "Reduced Shakespeare
Company" within the actual live performance of this
script is also EXPRESSLY PROHIBITED.

THE PLAY MUST BE BILLED AS FOLLOWS:

ALL THE GREAT BOOKS (abridged)
by
Reed Martin & Austin Tichenor

Additional Material by
Matthew Croke & Michael Faulkner

FOR WHAT IT'S WORTH

Although within the published script we use the name "Matt" for the student teacher character and Professor Tichenor for the drama teacher, the actors playing these roles in your production should be referred to by their actual first and last names. The third character is always simply referred to as "Coach." You can cast an actor with no actual first and last names if you so choose.

There are a number of topical references in the script. The humor and relevance of some of these will fade over time, so we encourage each production to keep these references as up-to-date as possible. This is not to say that scenes should be rewritten (which is, in fact, strictly prohibited) but rather we are giving you permission to change a punchline or reference from "Kato Kaelin" to "Paris Hilton," or from "Bill Clinton" to "George W Bush".

The production elements described in the script are from the original Reduced Shakespeare Company production. Consequently the scenery, props and costumes were all reduced in both quality and number. We'd encourage you to do the same. The conceit is not only that we are abridging All The Great Books, but everything within the production as well. There are only three actors and the setting is a high school theater. In theory, all the props and costumes in the show are being borrowed from the storage room of the high school drama department. It should look like you are flying by the seat of your pants and not like you've had months to come up with a fabulous design for the show. It's more charming if the whole thing looks like it's being made up on the spot.

In our experience, the script works best when it is performed simply and seriously. That is to say, the script is funny so play it straight. Keep the show moving. For God's sake, don't linger. Many of the punchlines are meant to be throwaways. And for those of you who think the whole script should be thrown away, we can only say we tried that and it didn't work nearly as well.

ACT ONE

(The scene is a high school auditorium. An American flag hangs from its pole S R. A white drawing board stands stage left; on it, "All The Great Books" is written in black marker.)

(The scenery is a backdrop painted as a library: floor-to-ceiling shelves covered with Great Books. Framed portraits and busts of Great Authors decorate the shelves.)

(There are two doors, right and left of upstage center, a real bookshelf between the two doorways, and a chair.)

(The pre-show music finishes with a very loud song, in the midst of which we hear a school bell ring, followed by a coach's whistle. COACH enters from the back of the house. He wears long athletic shorts, tall tube socks, baseball cap, a whistle, a stopwatch and carries a bag full of various sports balls.)

COACH: *(Talking over the loud music)* Alright everybody, settle down. Stop your private conversations. Put your personal items away. Turn off the radio!

(The music stops.)

COACH: Thank you. I'd like to welcome you to class, my name is... *(He writes on the board.)* ...Coach. Now we all know why we're here. This is a repeat course for those of you who didn't pass your Western Literature requirement last term. The School Board and Superintendant Wilcox require that you pass this course in order to graduate. Graduation is in one hour and forty-five minutes. *(He starts his stopwatch.)* Before we go any further, I've been asked to make a few announcements. *(He pulls a piece of paper out of his cap and reads.)* There is a varsity basketball game tonight in the gym at seven-thirty against the opponents. Advanced Placement Tests are scheduled for Saturday morning at nine A M. *(Looks over the audience)* Probably doesn't apply to anyone here. Today's hot lunch is sloppy joes and peach cobbler. The vegetable is ketchup. And now ladies and gentlemen, without further ado, all the great books.

(Eighty-nine books [Well, it's supposed to be eighty-nine but you can use less; no one's going to count them; we suggest throwing on thirty-six books, three of which have actual pages. The rest have the pages removed and replaced with foam. This makes them less likely to fall apart when they get thrown around] fly on from the right wing and crash to the floor.[They've been thrown by the other two actors.])

(PROFESSOR runs on. He wears glasses, a pink sweater vest, bow tie, and slacks.)

PROFESSOR: How was it?

COACH: A little bit much I thought.

PROFESSOR: The great books need a great entrance. I thought it was very theatrical.

COACH: Yes, well, you would. I'm sure all of you know Mister Tichenor, our drama teacher.

PROFESSOR: *(With a Shakespearean flourish)* I am but a humble player...

COACH: *(Trying to go on)* Yes...

PROFESSOR:...who struts and frets his hour upon the stage and is heard no more.

COACH: That would be great idea. Now, you may also be aware that our regular literature teacher was tragically trampled to death at a J K Rowling book signing. Since no one else was available on such short notice to teach the course, we eagerly volunteered.

PROFESSOR: We leapt at the chance.

COACH: Yes, we were thrilled. *(Remembering)* Oh, Superintendant Wilcox is requiring the Pledge of Allegiance.

PROFESSOR: Coach, I don't think we should.

COACH: Why not?

PROFESSOR: I have some trouble with that word.

COACH: "God"?

PROFESSOR: No, *invidisable.*

COACH: Apparently. Okay. If everyone would please rise to their feet to say the Pledge of Allegiance. Jehovah's Witnesses may remain seated. Put your right hand over your heart. We will say this in unison.

(Everyone has risen. They all speak in unison with COACH *and* PROFESSOR *leading.)*

COACH/PROFESSOR: I pledge allegiance to the flag of the United States of America. And to the Republic for which it stands, one nation, this phrase optional, indivisible (PROFESSOR *stumbles over this.*), with liberty and justice for all. Forever and ever, amen.

COACH: You may be seated. Jehovah's Witnesses may stand up.

(MATT runs on, carrying a book. He wears cargo pants, T-shirt covered by an unbuttoned Hawaiian shirt, and backwards baseball cap.)

MATT: Sorry! Sorry I'm late! Sorry students, sorry I'm late.

COACH: You should be. I'm sure many of you know our very late student teacher, Matt.

MATT: *(To audience)* Woo!

COACH: Where were you?

MATT: *(Revealing the book)* Reading *Lord of the Rings*, baby! Man, can you believe they made a book out of the movie?

COACH/PROFESSOR: MATT!

MATT: I just wanna say that you students are very lucky. When I went to school here, I didn't have great teachers like Coach or Mister Tichenor.

PROFESSOR: Matthew, please. Mister Tichenor is my father. Please, call me Professor.

COACH: *(To* MATT, *re: the books)* Straighten these up.

(MATT *exits to get a large push broom. He quickly reenters and begins to sweep all the books into a pile downstage.)*

COACH: So, students. What do we mean by "The Great Books"? Anyone? No? Well, I'm not surprised. And this is exactly why we're holding class in the school theater. It's the only room on campus large enough to accommodate this many remedial students.

PROFESSOR: And being in the school theatre will allow us to dramatize all the great books using my extensive collection of props and costumes, as well as— *(He gestures to the backdrop.)* The backdrop from my controversial production of *The Music Man*.

COACH: Now this is an awful lot of material to cover in a very short period of time because, as you can see, all the great books are here. *Ulysses. The Iliad. The Odyssey. Remembrance of Things Past. Moby Dick. Don Quixote.* Charles Dickens. And of course...

(MATT *drops one huge book—approximately 2' X 1' X 6" in size—on the floor. BANG! [It was preset on the bookshelf up-center.] All three bounce slightly from the vibration.)*

COACH: *War and Peace.*

PROFESSOR: If you could all take a look at your syllabus, which is in the handout you received on your way in, you'll notice we won't be covering *every* great book.

COACH: No, only the eighty-six *greatest* books.

(The three teachers have pulled out syllabi and refer to them.)

MATT: Wait a second, wait a second. *Lord of the Rings* isn't on here.

COACH: Nope. Nor is *The Communist Manifesto*.

PROFESSOR: That's right. No fantasy. But there's still plenty of material on here familiar to everyone. In fact, could I see by a show of hands, how many of you have ever read anything by Mister Charles Dickens? Charles Dickens, anyone? America's greatest—oh perfect.

(Many hands have been raised)

PROFESSOR: That's a wonderful place to start.

COACH & MATT: Great! *(They run off.)*

PROFESSOR: Now, our goal is to make these great works of literature come alive for you. And as your drama teacher, and the proud holder of an A A degree in theater— *(Picking a book from the floor)* —from *(Insert name of sub-par local technical or community college here; if the audience applauds or cheers this, PROFESSOR can say "I see some of you have been accepted there this fall".)*, the only way I know to make literature come alive is through the magic of theatre! And that's why I love Charles Dickens. *(Flipping through the pages)* Each of his novels is filled with exaggerated characterizations, action-packed plots, and cliffhanger endings. And so to give you a taste of the anticipation and drama experienced by the 19th century reader, we are proud to present to you Charles Dickens' continuing soap opera— *(Soap opera music begins.)* *Great Expectorations.* Brought to you by Tidy Kid. Four out of five indentured child laborers prefer Tidy Kid over the

second leading brand. Tidy Kid. It beats a beating.
And now, Episode Seventeen of *Great Expectorations:
A Sale of Two Titties.* Charles Darnay, trapped in prison,
is being interrogated by the evil Madame Defarge.

*(COACH and MATT enter as their characters are introduced.
COACH wears handcuffs and kneels center. MATT wears a
skirt and wig. PROFESSOR exits.)*

MATT/MADAME DEFARGE: It is the best of times.

COACH/DARNAY: It is the worst of times.

MATT/MADAME DEFARGE: Like sands through the
hourglass...

COACH/DARNAY:These are the *Days Of Our Lives.*

MATT/MADAME DEFARGE: You will not live to see
another day, Monsieur Darnay. You French Aristocrats
have destroyed Pine Valley! But we, the Bold and the
Beautiful are now the Young and the Restless! Our day
has come!

COACH/DARNAY:You must recant your lies so that I
can return to my loving wife Lucie Manette and our
four little ones.

MATT/MADAME DEFARGE: Ha! There are no longer
four. We have already executed Jean-Renault.

COACH/DARNAY:You shot J R?

MATT/MADAME DEFARGE: *Oui!*

(They exit. The PROFESSOR enters.)

PROFESSOR: Meanwhile, on the other side of the English
Channel in London, we see Oliver Twist.

(MATT enters dressed as OLIVER TWIST.)

MATT/OLIVER: Come on, baby, let's do the—

PROFESSOR/BOSS: Stop dancing, Oliver! Get back to
work!

(PROFESSOR *exits.* MATT *cleans the floor with his shirttail and bottle of cleanser.*)

MATT/OLIVER: It's a hard knock life. Lucky for me, I'm using Tidy Kid. *(He turns the bottle upside down, indicating that it's empty.)* Please, sir, may I have some more?

(COACH *enters as* SCROOGE *in night shirt and night cap.*)

COACH/SCROOGE: Bah, humbug.

MATT/OLIVER: Then may I leave early, sir? It's Christmas Eve.

COACH/SCROOGE: I suppose you'll want Christmas day off, as well.

MATT/OLIVER: If it's convenient.

COACH/SCROOGE: It is not convenient!

MATT/OLIVER: If you don't give me the time off, I'll be forced to reveal your dark secret to all the Desperate Housewives!

(Organ sting)

COACH/SCROOGE: Which dark secret?

(Sting)

MATT/OLIVER: That you and Jacob Marley were more than just business partners!

(We hear the famous baseball game organ chords, exhorting the crowd to yell, "Do do do do do-do". COACH and MATT both do a slight pelvic thrust in time to the music then exit. The PROFESSOR enters, and more soap opera music plays through his next speech.)

PROFESSOR: Will Charles Darnay escape from prison? Will Oliver star in a Broadway musical? Will Scrooge and Marley get married in San Francisco? The answer to these and other questions will be found next week in Episode Eighteen of *Great Expectorations*, when we see

David Copperfield date a German supermodel and
make the Statue of Liberty disappear.

*(Blackout as the music swells. The lights come up as the
music goes out and* COACH *and* MATT *enter.)*

MATT: That was great. In that last section we covered—
(Picks up four books) Dickens, Dickens, Dickens, Dickens,
and—

(PROFESSOR *tosses his book to* MATT*)*

MATT: Dickens! Five books down, eighty-one more to
go. *(He carries the books upstage and places them on the
bookshelf.)*

PROFESSOR: Very good. I'd like to move on now to the
Great Poets.

COACH: *(Starting to go)* Great.

MATT: Oh, I can help with this! *(Recites)*
"I will not do it in a boat.
I will not do it with a goat..."

COACH/PROFESSOR: Matt!

PROFESSOR: Matthew, I know Doctor Seuss makes
reading fun, but as we'll see, reading and fun have
very little to do with literature.

(COACH *exits. During his previous line,* PROFESSOR *has
searched his pockets unsuccessfully for his papers.)*

PROFESSOR: Shoot, I left my papers—

MATT: Oh, I'll get them, Professor. *(He exits.)*

PROFESSOR: Thank you, Matthew. You see, I've made it
my life's work to create a collection of the world's great
poems. And as well-read members of society, you need
to be familiar with such luminary poets as Yeats, Keats,
Longfellow, Tennyson, Maya Angelou, T S Eliot,
Walt Whitman, The Brothers Gibb...

(MATT *runs on, hands several sheets of paper to* PROFESSOR.*)*

MATT: There you go, Professor. *(He goes to the bookcase to straighten up.)*

PROFESSOR: Ah, thank you, Matthew. Ladies and gentlemen, my humble collection of the World's Great Poems. *(Clears his throat and begins to declaim)* "Toilet paper, extra large Vaseline Intensive Care hand lo—" What is this?

(MATT runs down to him.)

MATT: No, no! Don't read that. That's my shopping list. Professor do me a favor, do not read that! *(He exits.)*

PROFESSOR: Matthew, this is not what I need. I need my collection of poems. *(As he says this, he rips the pages three times and tosses them in the air.)*

MATT: *(O S)* Your collection of poems is on the back!

(PROFESSOR stares at the papers fluttering to the floor, as the lights shift to a spotlight on him.)

PROFESSOR: Don't worry. It's all up here. *(He taps his head, then stands there for a surprisingly long moment, convinced that something will come to him. Finally, something does.)* There once was a man from Nantucket

(The audience laughs. PROFESSOR goes on, making it up as he goes.)

PROFESSOR: Whose string was so long he could pluck it
He shot an arrow in the air
It fell to earth, there's no there there
And in the depths of his despair cried, "Fff—
(He catches himself and finds a different F-word to say.)
—fie on the person who put me here
In the Ballad of Reading Gaol *(Pronounced "Redding Jail")*
Where each man kills the thing he loves
And loves the thing he nails.
(He realizes that was horribly wrong.)
Oh...Captain! My Captain! *(He slowly drops to one knee, trying to pick up a paper scrap without being seen.)*

We go down to the sea in ships
*(He stands confidently, reading the only line on the tiny
scrap of paper.)*
The rhyming ancient mariner stormed the beach!
*(He realizes he's got nothing—again. He drops to his knee
to search for scraps and remembers another phrase.)*
"Beware the Jabberwock, my son
Who dares to part his hair behind
*(He finds two other scraps and reads triumphantly from one
of them.)*
And in Xanadu did Kubla Khan dare to eat a—
(Switching to the other scrap)
Peach, bananas, cucumbers...
*(He realizes he's reading from the wrong side of the paper.
He flips it over and continues, getting on a roll.)*
Lettuce go, then, you and I
When evening is spread out amongst the sky
Sky light burning bright
First star I see tonight
Rage rage against the dying of the light
(Standing triumphantly)
Do not go gentle into Gladys Knight!
Two roads diverged in a wood today
How do I love thee? Let me count the way
And I think that I shall never see
A poem as lovely as Doris Day
(Or Green Day, depending on the age of your audience)
Into the valley of the dolls rode the six hundred
On the eighteenth of April in seventy-five
Seventy-six trombones led the big parade
And I was stayin' alive, stayin' alive
O body swayed to music, O brightening glance
How can we know the dancer from the dance?
I know why the caged bird sings the body electric
Like a maniac, a maniac
(He kneels.)
On the floor!

'Cause there is no joy in Mudville
Now that Casey knows the score
Mighty Casey and
The Sunshine Band
Quoth the raven, "Baltimore". Thank you.

(He nods his head humbly. COACH *and* MATT *re-enter,
applauding. The lights come up.)*

MATT: Wow! Good save, Professor.

PROFESSOR: Not much of a "collection". More of a
"medley", really.

MATT: No, no, well done, man. Totally excrement.

PROFESSOR: Thank you.

MATT: You know, I hate to bring this up but I'm a little
concerned that this course is focusing only on dead
white men.

PROFESSOR: That's a fair concern, Matthew, but don't
worry. Next semester I'll be teaching a course on
"The Great Works by Trans-Gendered Lesbian Authors
of Color." Please sign up, it'll be held upstairs in the
broom closet.

COACH: And class, I encourage you, please do not be
prejudiced against the dead. Dead people have written
great books. In fact, L Ron Hubbard comes out with a
new one every year, so...

PROFESSOR: That's right. So don't be corpsist. And
secondly, Alexander Dumas is on our syllabus. And
he wasn't white, he was black.

MATT: Professor, please! Don't say "black." Say
"African-American."

PROFESSOR: But he was French.

MATT: Then say, "Franco-American."

PROFESSOR: Okaay. Alexander Dumas: the author of *The Three Musketeers, The Count of Monte Cristo* and apparently the inventor of Spaghetti-Os. But my point is, Dumas was not white—ah! *(Remembering)* And neither was Homer.

MATT: That's right. Homer's yellow. And his wife had big blue hair. And small little—

COACH & PROFESSOR: Matt!

PROFESSOR: Not *that* Homer. Homer, the Greek poet. Many scholars now believe that Homer was African. *African*-African. At the very least he was Greek, so he was dark and swarthy-looking. Well, he was from Greece, so he was Greece-y. Like Italians!

COACH/MATT: Mister Tichenor!/Professor!

PROFESSOR: *(Completely flustered)* Ah, I—look, I don't want to talk about skin color, I want to focus on the work! But since we're on the subject, I'll grant you that James Joyce was an Irish cream and Leo Tolstoy a white Russian. But Lady Murasaki is obviously not a dead white man. She was the Japanese noblewoman who in the tenth century wrote *The Story of Ghenji*, the world's first novel.

(COACH heads to the board and erases everything on it.)

COACH: The second-best book on the syllabus was written by a woman.

MATT: Who's that, Coach?

COACH: Louisa May Alcott.

PROFESSOR: You think *Little Women*'s a good book?

COACH: *Au, contraire mon petite fromage. Little Women* is a great book. Now in the book *Little Women*, the mother is named Marmee—which is short for "marmalade," because she's an extremely sweet woman, as well as the coach and general manager, and she's assembled a very strong team... *(Across the top of the board he writes the first initials of the following names on the board.)* ...with Meg, Amy, Beth, Edith, Tamara, Venus, Serena, and Flo Jo—the book's narrator. As the novel begins, the Little Women have lost their best player, their father... *(He writes a small "F")* ...to free agency. The Civil War has broken out and like everyone else he's signed with the Yankees. The Little Women are now a player down. Fortunately, the boy Laurie lives next door. *(He writes an "L")* He's an orphan, a free agent. The Little Women sign him and the league allows it because, let's face it, Laurie —girl's name. At this point the Little Women get two pieces of bad news. First they learn that Beth... *(He circles the letter "B" and then draws a downward line, at the end of which he draws a circle.)* ...has run a down-and-out to help the down and out family down the street whose infant has scarlet fever. Beth herself catches scarlet fever and is penalized fifteen yards.... *(He draws eyes and a frown inside the circle to make it a sad face.)* ...and her life. *(He makes an "X" across the sad face, crossing it out.)* They also learn that their father has taken ill and been placed on the Disabled List. At this point the Little Women reacquire the Father, nurse him back to health by pumping him full of steroids... *(He draws a huge exaggerated "F" over the smaller one he drew earlier.)* ...and he goes on to hit seventy-three home runs, as the Little Women win the World Series. *(He writes "Win" on the board.)* Now, the Little Women are so successful because their four best players are Meg, Amy, Edith and Tamara. *(He writes the first initials of these four names from last to first, so they spell out the word "Team.")* That's right. There's no "I" in "Team," no "U" in "Win." And all the Little Women live happily ever after. *(He draws the "female" sign on the board [The circle with a "+" at the bottom] and then turns it into a happy face.)* I thank you.

(PROFESSOR *shakes* COACH's *hand.* MATT *runs on wearing a beat-up, straw farmer's hat.*)

MATT: Yee-haw!! I'm gonna take my raft down the Mississippi River!

COACH: Woah! Matt, we're not doing *Huck Finn!*

MATT: What are you talking about? Ernest Hemingway said that all American literature stems from *Huckleberry Finn!*

PROFESSOR: He's right, Coach. And *Huckleberry Finn* is excellent source material for dramatization.

COACH: Yes, but we don't have the right people for *Huck Finn.*

MATT: We don't have the right people for any of these books.

COACH: No, you're missing my point. Who's gonna play Jim?

MATT: I don't know. Why don't you play Jim? You're big.

COACH: I'm not black.

MATT: Oh my god, that is so racist!

PROFESSOR: No, it isn't.

MATT: Yes, it is. He just denied himself an opportunity because of his race!

COACH: No, Jim was African-American. He was a runaway slave, not a runaway Scottish-German-Presbyterian. (*Indicating himself. The actor playing this role should say his own actual ethnicity and religion.*)

MATT: What kind of logic is that? C'mon Professor, you've heard of color-blind casting, haven't you?

PROFESSOR: You forget, I directed the first all-white production of *Ain't Misbehavin'*. So you can play Jim.

COACH: Okay, I'll agree to play Jim if you two agree to be true to the original language.

PROFESSOR: Absolutely.

MATT: Why else would you do it?

(PROFESSOR *and* MATT *start to exit.)*

COACH: So we'll be saying the "N" word?

PROFESSOR: Yes.

MATT: The what?

COACH: The "N" word.

MATT: Enron?

COACH: No, that's the "F" word. The "N" word.

(He whispers it to MATT.)

MATT: Oh my god, that is so racist!

PROFESSOR: No, it isn't.

MATT: Did you just hear what he said?!

COACH: I didn't call anybody that, I wasn't referring to anybody. We were having a class discussion, and in that context I'm perfectly comfortable saying it right out loud. You know....

(He whispers it behind his hand to MATT.)

MATT: Oh, my god! Stop saying that.

PROFESSOR: Matthew, Huck says that word. It's in the book.

MATT: That word is in the book?

PROFESSOR: Yes, it's accurate nineteenth century derogatory slang.

MATT: *(To the class)* Well, then you can cross *Huckleberry Finn* off your syllabus. We're not going to cover it. That book is racist.

PROFESSOR: No!

MATT: Yes!

PROFESSOR: Matthew, depicting racism is not racist. That's why we should study the book. Because it shows Huck's growing awareness of and then rejection of racism.

MATT: Yeah, but I am not comfortable with that word. Coach, I'm not comfortable with any ethnic labels.

COACH: But if we don't use ethnic labels, what do we call them?

MATT: "Them"? "Them"?! How about calling them people? Or fellow human beings?!

COACH: Calling who?

MATT: Them! Them! Don't make generalizations based on race. Argh! All white people do that.

(COACH *and* PROFESSOR *look at* MATT, *then continue.*)

PROFESSOR: You know, speaking of ethnic labels, did you know that in England black people are not called African-Americans?

COACH: Really?

MATT: All right. Can we please stop talking about this?

PROFESSOR: Oh, you know what they call underwear in England?

COACH: No.

MATT: Stop talking about black people.

PROFESSOR: Knickers.

COACH: Oh!

MATT: Oh my god, that's so racist! (*He begins to leave.*)

COACH: Oh, you know what they call a sausage in England?

PROFESSOR: No.

MATT: I'm calling my wife. *(He starts to leave again.)*

COACH: Banger.

PROFESSOR: Right.

MATT: Hey! I said *call* my wife!

PROFESSOR: You know what they call a cigarette in England?

COACH: Yep.

MATT: I'm calling my mom! *(Still trying to leave)*

PROFESSOR & COACH: Fag!

MATT: Hey! That was one time! In college! And I was drunk! *(Slowly, he realizes he may have revealed too much.)*

PROFESSOR: What, you smoked a cigarette?

MATT: Afterwards. Look, I don't understand how my personal life got on the syllabus. Can we please get back to *Huckleberry Finn*? The story of America, an adolescent country dealing with its ethics, morality, coming of age and in the end ultimately finding redemption?

(Beat)

PROFESSOR: Wow. That is an excellent summation of *Huckleberry Finn*.

MATT: Wow! You don't have to be so surprised, Professor!

PROFESSOR: I'm sorry. It's just that, basically, I've always thought you were illiterate.

(MATT charges the PROFESSOR, who runs away. COACH restrains MATT.)

MATT: I'll rip your head off!

COACH:Hey, Matt, calm down!

MATT: I am not illiterate! My parents were married!

PROFESSOR: I didn't mean you were born out of wedlock, I meant you can't read or write.

MATT: Course I can read and write! Just because I'm a student teacher doesn't make me a *total* idiot.

PROFESSOR: All right, I'm sorry I called you illiterate.

MATT: You should be! You should also be sorry for this, ah-ha! *(He pulls a book out of the back his pants.)* I found this in the garbage!

PROFESSOR: What is it?

MATT: It's Walden by Henry David Thoreau and *you* threw it away!

PROFESSOR: Oh, I did not!

(PROFESSOR *exits. [The scene continues on page 20.] But, if there's something political going on in the news, you can do this Breakdown Section. In this scenario,* PROFESSOR *doesn't say his "I didn't mean you were born out of wedlock..." line. Instead, he hides behind the American flag after* MATT's *"My parents were married" line, and it goes like this:)*

MATT: Just because I'm a student teacher doesn't make me... Stop that. What are you—? Come out of...stop hiding behind the flag.

PROFESSOR: *(Stepping out)* I don't know. It seems to be working for President Bush. *(Or whichever politician is deflecting criticism by questioning other people's patriotism.)*

MATT: Stop that...

(The audience will have a mixed response to this. To gauge whether he's gone too far, PROFESSOR *can simulate a laugh-meter with his arms.)*

MATT: Hey, you guys are the teachers. I guess you can go wherever you want.

PROFESSOR: *(Back in character)* All right, I'm sorry
I called you illiterate.

MATT: *(Thrown)* No, uh. You...hmm...what?
*(He tries to pick up the scene from where it left off,
but can't remember what he's supposed to say.)*

COACH:I guess because we're the teachers, that explains
why we know where we are.

(The audience laughs. MATT *has to acknowledge that*
COACH *got him, but still defend himself.)*

MATT: *(Sotto voce)* All right. Okay. But he said that,
you said that already.

PROFESSOR: *(Sotto voce)* I said it but I didn't apologize
for it...

COACH: *(Sotto voce)* Matt, pull the book out of your
pants.

MATT: What? Right. Skip it. *(Pulls book from the back of
his pants)* Aha! Look what I found!

PROFESSOR: Where'd you pull that out from? Is that
where you're hiding the weapons of mass destruction?

MATT: Stop it! I'm trying to get back to the... Ah-ha!
Look what I found in the—

COACH: *(To the audience, leading the applause)*
Matt Croke, ladies and gentlemen!

MATT: No, come on, stop. There's a rhythm to this,
guys, a rhythm!

COACH: *(Looking at his watch)* Not for the last fifteen
minutes.

MATT: I found this in the garbage! Yeah, I'm really mad
now!

PROFESSOR: What is it?

MATT: Oh, you know what it is! It's *Walden* by Henry David Thoreau, and you threw it away.

PROFESSOR: I did not.

(PROFESSOR exits. And now you're back to the script.]

MATT: Oh my gosh. Coach, Professor threw Walden in the garbage.

COACH: Professor didn't throw Walden in the garbage, I did. Because absolutely nothing happens in that book.

MATT: But this is Walden. It's a great book!

COACH:Well...

MATT: In fact, I have an action packed interpretation that I do with a subtle beauty.

COACH: Well, it's on the syllabus but make it quick.

(MATT hands the book to COACH and goes to grab the chair.)

COACH: Ladies and gentlemen, finally, an action packed, subtle interpretation of Henry David Thoreau's *Walden*.

(The lights shift. MATT has moved the chair downstage and sits on it, in a spotlight. We hear gentle music and sounds of crickets and sparrows. MATT sits very still. After awhile, he swats away an imaginary fly. Then he picks up an imaginary fishing pole and mimes casting the line into the pond. Suddenly COACH blows his whistle. The lights bounce back up.)

COACH: *(Using the actual football referee signals for "Personal Foul" and "Intentional Grounding")* Personal foul. Intentionally boring.

MATT: What are you talking about?

COACH: Yeah, there's a subtle beauty. So subtle I can't see it.

MATT: What could be more exciting than *Walden* by Henry David Thoreau?

COACH: *Walden* by Ernest Hemingway.

(COACH *slaps the book into* MATT's *chest. The lights shift again to just the spotlight. We again hear the gentle music and sounds of crickets and sparrows.* COACH *turns his baseball cap backwards and sits in the chair. He mimes taking a flask out of his pocket and taking a deep drink. He tosses the flask aside. Then he mimes casting and fishing. The pole breaks, so* COACH *mimes grabbing a rifle. He shoots toward the wings.* MATT *runs on carrying a very large bucket and large stuffed fish. He deliberately sets down the bucket, drops the fish in it and exits.* COACH *is puzzled, but then takes aim at something overhead and shoots. A second large fish falls from the sky and drops directly into the bucket.* COACH *looks at the audience and raises one eyebrow. Blackout. Lights up.* MATT *restores the chair.* PROFESSOR *enters checking his syllabus.*)

COACH: Guys, we need to pick up the pace here. We still have all these books to cover. I say we just jump right into *War and Peace. (He picks up the huge* War and Peace *book.)*

PROFESSOR: Woah! Coach, don't you think *War and Peace* is a little complicated?

COACH: What's complicated? It's just like every other Russian novel. The motherland is being invaded, the people are being persecuted, and the Russians are drunk off their ass. *(He slams the huge* War and Peace *book shut and sets it back down on the floor.)*

MATT: You know what? Nobody knows the Russian novels. Why don't we cover a book that everybody has read?

PROFESSOR: Good thinking, Matthew. Here's one I'm sure you all know. *(Picking one off the floor)* How many of you have read *Don Quixote*?

(The three performers raise their hands, indicating that anyone who has read Don Quixote *should raise theirs. Hardly anyone does.)*

COACH: Seven.

MATT: What?

PROFESSOR: Come on! You must know the musical *Man of La Mancha. (Singing very, very badly)* To dream, the impossible—!

MATT & COACH: *(Various)* Woah! Hey! Stop!

COACH: Mister Tichenor, that's okay!

PROFESSOR: But I love that song!

COACH: Well then learn the tune.

PROFESSOR: *Don Quixote*'s a great story about an old man who imagines himself to be a knight errant. Where we see windmills, Don Quixote sees giants.

COACH: Where we see prostitutes, he sees princesses.

MATT: Where we see Jim Carrey, he sees Antonio Banderas.

COACH/PROFESSOR: *Si!*

*(*PROFESSOR *tosses* MATT *the book, which* MATT *places on the bookshelf upstage as he and* COACH *exit.* PROFESSOR *moves up near the door as he speaks.)*

PROFESSOR: *Don Quixote* is an exquisite story all about the power of the imagination! In Don Quixote's world, this tattered robe—

(From offstage someone throws PROFESSOR *a worn-out looking bathrobe. He catches it and puts it on.)*

PROFESSOR: —becomes a magnificent suit of armor. And this child's plaything—

(On flies a plastic pail, which he puts on his head, tucking the handle under his chin.)

PROFESSOR: —becomes a knight's helmet. Now in order for you to more fully appreciate the beauty inherent in Miguel de Cervantes' language, my extinguished colleague Coach will join me in performing *Don Quixote* in the original Spanish, while Matthew translates.

(MATT *enters and crosses to a spot D L.*)

MATT: Hola. *(He waves)* Hello. *(He waves)*.

(PROFESSOR *poses dramatically.*)

PROFESSOR/QUIXOTE: *Soy Don Quixote de la Mancha.*

MATT: I am Don Quixote of La Mancha.

PROFESSOR/QUIXOTE: *...el desachador de injusticia...*

MATT: ... the undoer of injustice...

PROFESSOR/QUIXOTE: *...el protector de doncellas...*

MATT: ...the protector of damsels...

PROFESSOR/QUIXOTE: *...y el terror de gigantes.*

MATT: ...and the terror of giants.

PROFESSOR/QUIXOTE: *Montaré mi magnifico caballo, Rocinante.*

MATT: I will ride on my magnificent horse, Rocinante.

(PROFESSOR *looks to the doorway, anticipating that he will be thrown a stick horse. But instead of being thrown onstage, the stick horse is "accidentally" thrown across the doorway and out of sight upstage. After a beat, we see an embarrassed stage hand cross the doorway to retrieve the stick horse. After another beat, the stage hand crosses back to their original position. Finally, PROFESSOR says...*)

PROFESSOR/QUIXOTE: Rocinante!

(*A hand holds out the stick horse from the doorway.* PROFESSOR *takes the horse and puts it between his legs, but with the horse's face facing up. He does a double-take at the horse and then turns the head so that it faces downward.*)

(COACH *enters, riding a mop like a stick donkey. He speaks with a heavy nasal Mexican accent.*)

COACH/SANCHO: *Hola, Señor Quixado. Me llamo Sancho Panza. Como esta?*

MATT: *(imitating his accent)* Good morning, Mister Quixado. My name is Sancho Panza. How are you?

PROFESSOR/QUIXOTE: *No soy Señor Quixado. Soy Don Quixote de la Mancha.*

MATT: I am not Mister Quixado. I am Don Quixote of La Mancha.

PROFESSOR/QUIXOTE: *Yo requiero un escudero fiel para mi pesquisa.*

MATT: I require a faithful squire for my quest.

PROFESSOR/QUIXOTE: *Me acompañas?*

MATT: Will you join me?

COACH/SANCHO:*No se.*

MATT: *(Exaggerating* COACH's *accent)* I'm not sure.

PROFESSOR/QUIXOTE: *Quiero hacer bien...*

MATT: I want to do right....

PROFESSOR/QUIXOTE: *...a los hechos malos...*

MATT: ...to right wrongs...

PROFESSOR/QUIXOTE: *...y impresionar Dulcinea...*

MATT: ...and to win the love of Dulcinea...

PROFESSOR/QUIXOTE: *...la chica con los melones mas grandes en Espana.*

(*He gestures, indicating large breasts.* MATT *is shocked and doesn't quite know how to translate this, but finally...*)

MATT: *(Repeating* PROFESSOR's *gesture)* ...the girl with the biggest hands in Spain.

COACH/SANCHO: *Si, te acompañares en tu sueño imposible.*

MATT: Yes, I will join you in your impossible dream.

COACH/SANCHO: *Pero tengo miedo que yo no pueda marchar al paso de un asno de este tamaño.*

MATT: But I'm afraid that I will not be able to keep pace with an ass of this size.

(PROFESSOR *and* MATT *look at* COACH's *behind.* COACH *turns and looks behind his back at the wall, then shrugs and continues.)*

COACH/SANCHO: *Y como fue que Mateo pudo hacer todo en ingles?*

MATT: And how come Matt gets to do the whole scene in English?

PROFESSOR/QUIXOTE: *Porque Mateo es estupido.*

(PROFESSOR *and* COACH *have a good laugh.)*

MATT: Because Matt is stupendous. *(Quickly repeating his waves)* Hola! Hello!

PROFESSOR/QUIXOTE: *Andale!*

MATT: Let's ride!

(PROFESSOR *and* COACH *"ride" in a half circle around the stage.* PROFESSOR *makes horse noises,* COACH *makes donkey sounds.* MATT *slaps his chest to make galloping sounds.)*

PROFESSOR/QUIXOTE: *Alto.*

MATT: Stop!

PROFESSOR/QUIXOTE: *Mira, amigo Sancho! Gigantes!*

MATT: Look, friend Sancho! Giants!

COACH/SANCHO: *Usted es loco. Todo lo que veo son molinos de viento.*

MATT: You are delusional, my friend. All I see are windmills.

PROFESSOR/QUIXOTE: *No estoy loco!*

MATT: Sanity is overrated!

COACH/SANCHO: *Pardoname.*

MATT: I'm sorry.

COACH/SANCHO: *Mi mal.*

MATT: My bad.

PROFESSOR/QUIXOTE: *Gracias.*

MATT: Thank you.

COACH: *(Very angrily, to* MATT*)* They know what *gracias* means.

MATT: *(Imitating* COACH, *very angrily)* Saben que quiere decir "*gracias*".

*(*COACH *and* PROFESSOR *turn slowly and stare angrily at* MATT. MATT *shrugs as if to say, "What? They liked it."*

PROFESSOR/QUIXOTE: *Tengo que atacar! Ha, ha!*

MATT: I must attack! Hee, hee!

*(*PROFESSOR *rides through the doorway. We hear and see bits of a struggle.* PROFESSOR*'s head sticks out and a huge green toy Hulk hand grabs it and pulls it back. [In fact, he himself is wearing the green toy Hulk hand.] Then the stick horse's head sticks out and looks at the audience with a confused Scooby sound. The hand appears and pulls the head back with a loud "Zoinks!" Then* PROFESSOR *crosses past the doorway with his own hands around his throat.)*

PROFESSOR/QUIXOTE: *Oh, dios mio!*

MATT: Oh, my god.

(Now PROFESSOR *passes back across the doorway, dragging himself by his own pink sweater vest. As he disappears there's a loud thud.)*

PROFESSOR/QUIXOTE: *(O S) Oh, mi cajones!*

MATT: Oh, my testicles.

(PROFESSOR *stumbles back on, cradling his crotch.*)

COACH/SANCHO: *Como estas, Don Quixote?*

PROFESSOR/QUIXOTE: *No muy bueno.*

MATT: *(As* COACH*) How are you, Don Quixote?*
(As PROFESSOR, *high-pitched)* Not very well.

COACH/SANCHO: *Tu viste una pelea falsa contigo mismo de fuera del escenario.*

MATT: You had a very phony fight with yourself offstage.

PROFESSOR/QUIXOTE: *No es phonisimo. Es muy realistico.*

MATT: It was not phony. It was very realistic.

PROFESSOR/QUIXOTE: *Estaba peliando con gigantes...*

MATT: I was battling giants...

PROFESSOR/QUIXOTE: *...en las planos de España.*

MATT: ...on the plains of Spain.

COACH/SANCHO:*Donde hay lluvia?*

MATT: Where the rain mainly stays?

(COACH *smiles to the audience at his own cleverness.*)

PROFESSOR: *(Not amused)* Hijo de puta.

(MATT's *instantly shocked.* COACH *doesn't know what it means and looks at* MATT *for the translation.*)

MATT: *(Struggling for a family-friendly way to traslate this)* He questions Sancho's heritage.

(COACH *is angered.*)

PROFESSOR/QUIXOTE: *Chinga té!*

(COACH *again looks to* MATT *for the translation.*)

MATT: *(Still struggling)* And tells him to perform a physical impossibility on himself.

PROFESSOR/QUIXOTE: *(Referring to the mop donkey)*
Y tu burro, tambien.

MATT: And the horse he rode in on.

PROFESSOR/QUIXOTE: *Y tu! Chinga te, tambien!*

(He gives the "up yours" gesture to MATT, *and storms off.)*

MATT: *(Giving the "up yours" gesture to the audience)*
And he salutes me for all my work on this difficult
translation.

*(*COACH *follows the* PROFESSOR *off.)*

MATT: *Gracias. (He bows. He looks off.)* I hope Coach
doesn't hit the Professor. Coach is a great guy and all,
but he's got a bit of a temper, it's kind of legendary.
*(He waits for a beat, hoping they'll re-appear. When they
don't, he decides to take charge.)* Actually, you know what
will make him really mad? I used to do this when I
went to school here. This is great. *(He picks up a book.)*
Oh perfect—*Plato's Republic.* When Coach says the
word "Plato," everybody sneeze. Okay? This'll be great.
When you hear "Plato," sneeze. Got it? Now Coach
might get so upset that he'll forget to cover Plato, but
don't worry about it. I'll cover it for you now, just in
case. He's only one guy, how tough can it be? *(He flips
through the book. It looks incomprehensible so he figures it
must be upside down. He flips it over. Then he realizes he had
it right the first time and flips it back.)* Now we all know
that Plato wrote a lot of great books, but what he's
really best known for is that soft molding clay that
bears his name.

*(*COACH *re-enters.)*

COACH: Everything under control?

MATT: Yeah, Coach. Great class.

COACH: Sorry for the interruption, students. Mister
Tichenor?

(PROFESSOR *enters, holding a large ice pack to his crotch.*)

PROFESSOR: Sorry.

COACH: There we are. Is this the next book?

(MATT *hands him the Plato book.*)

MATT: Yes it is, Coach. All set.

COACH: *(Opening the book)* Ah yes. The great Greek philosopher, Plato.

(The class sneezes in unison.)

COACH: All right. Who's behind this?

PROFESSOR: Come on, Coach. You need to have a sense of humor about this sort of thing. Little scamps.

COACH: You know, you screw around for four years of high school... *(Picking someone specific, like a latecomer if there was one)* In some cases, seven years...

MATT: Coach, how about if I form a committee, and I'll find out who's behind this.

COACH: I like the way you think.

MATT: Yes sir!

COACH: *(Opening the book again)* Now, we all know that the great Greek philosopher Plato wrote a lot of....

(The class sneezes again. COACH *slams the book to the floor and tries to charge into the class.* PROFESSOR *and* MATT *restrain him.)*

COACH: This is ridiculous! I am trying to teach a class!

PROFESSOR: Coach, you need to learn to laugh at yourself.

MATT: Coach, c'mon. Besides, I've covered all this already.

PROFESSOR: Wait. You covered the great Greek philosopher Plato?!

(The class sneezes, with any luck. PROFESSOR *turns on them.)*

PROFESSOR: That's not funny.

MATT: *(To the class)* What is wrong with you people?
I said when Coach says it.

*(*COACH *and* PROFESSOR *slowly turn to look at him.)*

COACH: WHAT!?!?!

MATT: *(Covering)* That's right. I said when Coach says it,
you do it! If he says jump, you ask "How high?"

COACH: All right!

MATT: Yeah!

*(*COACH *and* MATT *high five.* MATT *hurts his hand. He
picks up the Plato book , places it on the bookshelf and exits.)*

PROFESSOR: Well, if Matthew's already covered Plato...

(If the class sneezes here, PROFESSOR *gives them a disdainful
"Stop it".)*

PROFESSOR: ...then the only ancient left on the syllabus
is my favorite author, the Greek poet Homer. Now,
Homer wrote and performed the two epics that are
the basis for all Western literature—*The Iliad* and
The Odyssey—which I have translated from the
original Greek into rhyming iambic septameter.

COACH: And class, I hope you appreciate that Mister
Tichenor's translation is by far the most accurate I have
ever read.

PROFESSOR: Really. You've read Homer?

COACH: Yeah.

PROFESSOR: In the original Greek?

COACH: No biggie.

PROFESSOR: You're a P E teacher and a Greek scholar?

COACH: Duh! I was in a fraternity.

PROFESSOR: So was I! I was in the existential fraternity.

COACH: Which one?

PROFESSOR: Signa Fi Nothing. Matthew!

(MATT *returns with three copies of the* PROFESSOR's *translation and hands one to* PROFESSOR *and one to* COACH.)

PROFESSOR/QUIXOTE: Thank you, Matthew. Now in my translation, you will perform the role of the great Greek warrior Achilles.

MATT: Awesome! Achilles! He's the...uh...

COACH: He's the hero of *The Iliad.*

MATT: Right! I love *The Iliad*...the epic story of—?

PROFESSOR: Of Achilles, who is sent off to rescue Helen of Troy and ultimately changes the course of the Trojan War.

MATT: Right, this'll be fun. Remind me again, what's his background?

PROFESSOR: Oh this is good. When Achilles was a baby, his mother dipped him into the River Styx...

MATT: That's terrible!

PROFESSOR: No, no—to make him invincible.

MATT: Awesome!

PROFESSOR: But she held him by the heel, which didn't get wet, so that part remained vulnerable. It's from this we get the term "Achilles heel".

MATT: So except for my heel, nobody can see me!

COACH/PROFESSOR: No! No!

(MATT *starts to act like* PROFESSOR *and* COACH *can't see him. He makes ghost sounds and pretends to float. He picks up a book and acts like it is floating on its own, then he carries it up to the doorway and drops it on the bookshelf. He exits.)*

COACH: *(Following* MATT *off)* I'll make sure he doesn't disappear.

PROFESSOR: Thank you. Now, this godfather of all literary journeys must begin with the traditional invocation to the Greek gods.

(He sticks the script in his pocket and claps his hands. The lights snap to a special. He adopts an invocation pose.)

PROFESSOR: Oh, muse of epic poetry, Calliope by name
Please grant my new translation with a measure of your fame
And help us understand Homer's *Iliad* and *Odyssey*
Through my humbly brilliant version, called "The Idioddity!"

(Dramatic music begins. PROFESSOR *exits as* COACH *enters. He reads his script.)*

COACH/CHORUS: Achilles was a soldier,
Agamemnon was his king
They both were given women,
which are very special things
But Agamemnon gave his back.
That's the kind of King he is.
And since he gave his back,
he thought Achilles should give him his.

*(*MATT *enters in* ACHILLES *breast plate. He carries a small spear.)*

MATT/ACHILLES: That is an insult! I won that woman fair and square! I'm Achilles! When I was a baby, I was dipped in the River Styx, now nobody can see me. I am invisible!

COACH/CHORUS: Achilles stopped participating in the Trojan War

MATT/ACHILLES: I do not hate the Trojans so what am I fighting for?

COACH/CHORUS: Athena then appeared, she was beautiful and mincing,

(PROFESSOR *"floats" on, in a wig and large hoop skirt. The skirt is floor length, so it covers his feet. He appears to be floating.*)

COACH/CHORUS: And here's what's kinda scary. He's surprisingly convincing. *(He exits.)*

PROFESSOR/ATHENA: Achilles, don't! Agamemnon is your king and fellow Greek!

MATT/ACHILLES: But he's insulted me and made me look feeble and weak!

PROFESSOR/ATHENA: You can't withdraw! He needs your skill to fight the Trojan War.

MATT/ACHILLES: Well, all that I can say is he shoulda thoughta that before.

(MATT *stabs the hoop skirt and exits. The hoop skirt starts to "deflate" like all the air is escaping from under it.*)

PROFESSOR: Ahhhhh! I'm melting, I'm MELTING! *(He "melts" slowly to the floor. When he gets as low as he can, he bows and exits.)* Thank you. *(And, thus, we cover* The Wizard of Oz.)

(COACH *enters.*)

COACH/CHORUS: Achilles couldn't help it. The Gods' mighty magic laws
Fueled his pride and anger.

(MATT *pops his head back out.*)

MATT/ACHILLES: I hate my tragic flaws!

COACH/CHORUS: Now comes Paris, the most hated person on the planet

(COACH *exits. The* PROFESSOR *enters in a beret, twirling a plastic sword.*)

PROFESSOR/PARIS: *(In an outrageous French accent)*
Ohh, ho, ho, ho! You know zat 'orrible Trojan War?
Well, I began it.
Zis is Helen of Troy, ze greatest beauty of our day.

(MATT enters as HELEN of Troy, with wig, skirt and feather boa.)

MATT/HELEN: My face launched a thousand ships!

PROFESSOR/PARIS: Zey couldn't wait to get away.
Zis whole war started when I stole her from Menolaos,
Which is why he and all ze Greeks now want to slay us.

(COACH enters with crown, plastic sword, and glasses.)

COACH/MENALAOS: I'm Menalaos. That's my wife.
Now what do you propose?

PROFESSOR/PARIS: A duel between us will bring years
of fighting to a close.

MATT/HELEN: And the winner of this battle gets to take
off all my clothes! *(He exits.)*

COACH/MENALAOS: I accept your challenge, and will
avenge what you did to me.

(They draw their swords.)

PROFESSOR/PARIS: If you want your wife back, sucker,
you will have to go right through me!

(MENALAOS lightly taps PARIS on the arm.)

PROFESSOR/PARIS: Ow! I'm hit! Great Zeus! I am feeling
very sickly! *(He exits.)*

COACH/MENALAOS: Leave it to a Frenchman to
surrender very quickly.

(COACH exits. MATT enters as CHORUS.)

MATT/CHORUS: And so the war continued, many
thousands more were dying. King Agamemnon
couldn't win—

(COACH *enters.* MATT *leaves.*)

COACH/AGAMEMNON: Hey, at least I'm trying!

(The PROFESSOR *enters, doing his own fanfare. He wears a blue t-shirt with a Greek "O" (Omega) sign on the front. It looks like the "S" logo that Superman wears. The shirt has a short red cape attached.)*

PROFESSOR/ODYSSEUS: I'm Odysseus, your highness,
let me go to Troy and check it.
I'll reconnoiter.

COACH/AGAMEMNON: Good. You find that noiter and
you wreck it! *(He exits.)*

PROFESSOR/ODYSSEUS: I will.
That night we crept to town and we made the Trojans
   blee-id
In the only section in this class you'll hear from *The
   Aeneid.*

(The class reacts to the bad rhyme. PROFESSOR *drops his*
ODYSSEUS *character.)*

PROFESSOR: All right, you just bought yourselves a
lecture. *The Aeneid* is the Roman poet Virgil's story of
the founding of Rome. It too tells the story of the Trojan
War, but more from a viewpoint of Roman nationalism.
The lesson here is that the Romans stole everything
from the Greeks, their gods, their myths, their salads.
So we're gonna skip all of *The Aeneid,* except for this
one famous section, which I'm sure you'll recognize.
(Back in character) I gathered all my men in a large and
rather coarse group
And entered through the main gate disguised as Trojan
Horse poop.

(He exits. Music plays. COACH *and* MATT *enter in a
vaudeville horse costume.* COACH *is the head;* MATT's
the rear end. They sneak around in time to the music.
PROFESSOR *enters as a guard who keeps looking for the*

horse, but not seeing it. Finally the guard spots the horse,
who hands the guard a scroll that says, "For The Trojans."
The guard shows the note to the audience, gestures to the
horse to follow him into the city, then skips offstage. The
horse does a little celebratory dance, finishing with step-kicks
and a bow. PROFESSOR *re-enters as* ODYSSEUS, *hiding*
upstage of the horse. He crawls underneath the horse and
speaks.)

PROFESSOR/ODYSSEUS: Once they got me in I couldn't
wait to go get started!
This really was a master plan

MATT: *(Taking off his part of the horse costume)* All right!
Who farted?

*(*MATT *exits.* COACH, *still wearing the horse head, does a*
slow take to the audience then sprints off. PROFESSOR *shakes*
his head: apparently this wasn't planned, and his anger fuels
the next line.)

PROFESSOR/ODYSSEUS:
This war really stinks. Achilles has to reconsider.
His selfishness has made him very angry, very bitter.

*(*PROFESSOR *exits as* MATT *enters.)*

MATT/ACHILLES:
Perhaps my foolish arrogance and pride was the cause.
I'll ask my trusted friend and adviser, Patroklos!
(Patra-Claus)

*(*COACH *enters as* PATROKLOS. *He wears a red Santa hat*
and white beard, but still has on the horse trousers. He holds
a plastic sword.)

COACH/PATROKLOS: Ho, ho, ho! Merry Iliad,
everybody! Hey, little fella have a seat. Tell old
Patroklos what you want for Christmas.

*(*MATT *sits on* COACH'*s knee and starts to say his next line,*
but taps COACH *on the chest with his spear, then catches his*

beard with the sword as he pulls it away. They both fall out of character.)

COACH: Ow! You're on the naughty list.

(He hits MATT's *breast plate with his sword, then notices that the armor is on back to front.)*

COACH: And your armor's on backwards, genius.

MATT: At least I managed to get out of my horse pants. Oops!

*(*COACH *looks down at the horse pants he is indeed still wearing and shakes his head. Then they get back to the scene.)*

MATT/ACHILLES: *(Back in character)* Be careful, Patroklos, there are spies in my house!

COACH/PATROKLOS: No, no! Not a creature is stirring, not even a mouse.

MATT/ACHILLES: My Greeks are getting killed out there. Have I been led astray? What can I do?

COACH/PATROKLOS:
My friend, I do believe there is a way!
Make a list, check it twice, kill the naughty, save the
    nice.
Let me wear your armor, everyone will think I'm you.
The troops will rally 'round me

MATT/ACHILLES: That's the perfect thing to do!

*(*COACH *puts on* MATT's *breast plate and begins to exit.)*

MATT/ACHILLES: And I heard him exclaim as he went off to fight...

COACH/PATROKLOS: Merry Battles to all, and to all a good— *(He screams half-heartedly from offstage.)* —God I'm being killed!

(The Santa hat and beard fly out from the doorway where COACH *exited.* MATT *falls to the ground in over-the-top emotional agony.)*

MATT/ACHILLES: Oh my God, I killed him! In Hell I will
be fried!

Patraklos is dead! I've committed Patra-cide!

(COACH *enters.)*

COACH/CHORUS: Achilles vows to end the war before
there dies another.
So he fights with Hektor...

(PROFESSOR *enters as* HEKTOR, *in the same beret that* PARIS
wore.)

COACH/CHORUS: ...Paris's older brother. The Trojan
War can be summed up by what they represent.

(COACH *exits.* ACHILLES *with his spear and* HEKTOR *with
his sword circle each other. They debate while they fight.*
MATT *fights like a tough guy.* PROFESSOR *is prissy.)*

MATT/ACHILLES: I'm primitive and brutal!

(MATT *lunges at* PROFESSOR.)

PROFESSOR/HEKTOR: I'm a civil government.

(PROFESSOR *attacks back.)*

MATT/ACHILLES: I'm undisciplined, instinctive.

(*He swings his spear at* PROFESSOR.)

PROFESSOR/HEKTOR: I am reason, self-control.

(PROFESSOR *kicks* MATT *in the groin.)*

MATT/ACHILLES: It's every man for himself.

PROFESSOR/HEKTOR: No... (*He slaps* MATT *on the head
with his sword.)* ...it's mankind as a whole.

MATT/ACHILLES: This fighting while debating makes
me frustrated and weary.

PROFESSOR/HEKTOR: My benevolent ways will win
out—

(MATT *stabs* PROFESSOR.)

PROFESSOR/HEKTOR: So much for that theory.

(They bow and exit, shaking hands as they go. COACH *enters.)*

COACH/CHORUS: The Trojan War was over, Achilles
   had no equal,
But The Iliad was such a hit Homer had to write a
   sequel.
When The Odyssey begins, ten more years have now
   gone by,
And Odysseus's son is one very wimpy guy.

*(*COACH *exits.* MATT *skips on as* TELEMACHUS, *wearing a beanie with propeller and licking an oversized lollipop. His voice cracks, like a boy whose voice is changing.)*

MATT/TELEMACHUS I am Telemachus and I don't know
   what to do.
My mother is besieged by men who all are pitching
   woo.

*(*PROFESSOR *and* COACH *lean their heads in one of the doorways. They hold flowers and heart-shaped boxes of candy. In unison they say...)*

BOTH: Telemachus, is your mom home?

(They both pant, tongues hanging out of their mouths. MATT *waves them off, and they pop out of sight.)*

MATT/TELEMACHUS: Go away!

BOTH: Aw!

MATT/TELEMACHUS: They want to marry Mom,
they think my father's not alive...

*(*PROFESSOR *"flies" into one doorway. He achieves this by bending at the waist and leaning into the doorway—hands in front of him, chest towards the floor. The audience can only see him only from the waist up.)*

PROFESSOR/ODYSSEUS: They might be right. I don't
appear in *The Odyssey* 'till Book Five. (*He does flying bits*

*in the doorway. He waves at the audience. He does a barrel
roll. He turns his body so that his chest is facing the audience
and moves up and down. He puts his hand to his brow,
looking towards the audience.)*

MATT: Professor, what are you doing?

PROFESSOR/ODYSSEUS: Just using my X-ray vision.

MATT: Professor, get out here and do Book Five.

*(PROFESSOR mimes shifting into reverse, and backs out of the
doorway. COACH makes backing-up beeping noises offstage.
PROFESSOR runs around backstage and leaps into the
doorway from the opposite side from which he backed up.
MATT exits.)*

PROFESSOR/ODYSSEUS: *(When audience doesn't react)*
No, no, hold your applause.
At the beginning of Book Five, I start my epic journey
But I am held as prisoner without trial or attorney
I'm trapped for seven years on the island of Calypso!

*(MATT re-enters as CALYPSO in wig, grass skirt, and
seashell bikini top.)*

MATT/CALYPSO: Day-O! Day-ay-ay-oh! The Gods have
told me to let you go!

*(MATT shimmies, showing the audience his shells and his
behind.)*

PROFESSOR/ODYSSEUS:
Oh Calypso, you turn me on you wild and wanton lass.
I see your sexy seashells and seductive shapely grass.
I must escape this island and begin my odyssey!

(He starts to go but MATT grabs him.)

MATT/CALYPSO: Only after one more night of sexuality!
(Trying to undress him) You're gonna get it boy, you
know it'll be fantastic.

PROFESSOR: Stop it, man, you're scaring me. You're too
enthusiastic.

(MATT *grabs a wooden slapstick—available at most music stores—from the bookshelf and makes* PROFESSOR *bend over at the waist.*)

MATT/CALYPSO: Assume the position like your Greek fraternal brother.

(*He spanks* PROFESSOR *with the slapstick, then exits.* PROFESSOR *backs upstage in the doorway as he speaks.*)

PROFESSOR: Thank you, lovely goddess. Please sir, may I have another?

(MATT'*s hand reaches into the doorway and pulls* PROFESSOR *offstage.* COACH *enters with a trident, wearing a snorkel, mask, and kid's safety float around his waist. The float looks like a turtle or something equally childish.*)

COACH/POSEIDON:
I am Poseidon. With my trident, I am God of water.
I am Zeus's brother, the little mermaid is my daughter.
The nymph has freed Odysseus from his sexual
    indenture
I think it's time I sent him on a Poseidon adventure!

(COACH *waves his trident.* PROFESSOR/ODYSSEUS *is pulled onstage and sent flying into the wings. As he crosses the stage he points at an audience member and says—*)

PROFESSOR/ODYSSEUS: Look! Ernest Borgnine!

(PROFESSOR *screams as he exits, as* MATT *enters to narrate.*)

MATT/CHORUS: How did Odysseus, wanting to get
    home despite the odds,
Manage to piss off one of the nastiest of Gods?
Let's find out. Odysseus washes up in foreign
territory—

(PROFESSOR "*washes up*" *onto the stage. Unbeknownst to the audience, he has a mouthful of water. Laying on his back, he spits some of it into the air like a fountain. It sprays people in the front row.*)

MATT/CHORUS: —and proceeds to tell the natives there his most amazing story.

(COACH *has entered as elderly Phaeacian* KING ALCINOUS. *He is hard of hearing and has an ear horn. He, too, has a mouthful of water unbeknownst to the audience. He uses one mouthful of water for this whole section.*)

(PROFESSOR *has gotten to his feet and now stands next to* COACH.)

(*Now* PROFESSOR *deliberately spits his mouthful of water into* COACH's *ear horn.* COACH *then turns and spits a mouthful of water in* MATT's *face. The illusion is that the water has gone through the ear horn, into* COACH's *mouth, and onto* MATT's *face.*)

PROFESSOR/ODYSSEUS: My friends, you have been
   gracious and hospitable to me
Let me tell you how I got here, how my story came to be
My horse maneuver worked, allowing us to win the
   war—

COACH/KING ALCINOUS: (*Yelling*) What did you feed it?

PROFESSOR/ODYSSEUS: Feed what?

COACH/KING ALCINOUS: (*Yelling*) Your horse. Please tell us some more.
How did horse manure keep your glory undiminished?

PROFESSOR/ODYSSEUS: Horse *maneuver*, Helen Keller,
   now shut up and let me finish.
We sailed away like a homesick bunch of lost romantics,
Past the Isle of Lesbos for some lovely lesbiantics.

COACH/KING ALCINOUS: (*Knowingly nudging* MATT *with his elbow.*) I can hear you now!

PROFESSOR/ODYSSEUS: We accidentally sailed off course
   by many miles and meters,
Then finally washed up upon the Land of Lotus-Eaters.
The people there were lovely and they greeted us with

hugs.
Even better, they also gave us mind-expanding drugs.

(Light change. We hear groovy sixties sitar music. COACH
and MATT *react as if stoned, then dance offstage.)*

PROFESSOR/ODYSSEUS: It was groovy, fab, and gear,
  a break from our long mission.
But then it took us over and it wiped out our ambition.
(He starts to channel William Shatner.)
We were acting strangely, poisoned by this magic
  potion.
Sulu took his shirt off and Spock finally showed
  emotion.
Then I grabbed Uhura and we danced an arabesque—
(He slaps his face several times to snap himself out of it.)
—but I struggled back to normal in a manner
  Shatner-esque.
We found a cave we thought would be a protected
  refuge

*(*MATT *enters.)*

PROFESSOR/ODYSSEUS: Until we saw the Cyclops!

*(*COACH *stomps on as the one-eyed* CYCLOPS. *He has a large
single fake eye on the top of his head.)*

COACH/CYCLOPS: Fee fi fo ...

MATT/SAILOR: Oh my God, that guy is huge!

(Using small dolls and high voices, MATT *and* PROFESSOR
*act this out. The dolls are dressed identically to the actors.
The dolls knock each other down in their panic.)*

MATT/AUSTIN: *(Various)* Run away! Let's get out of
here!

PROFESSOR/ODYSSEUS: Greetings, giant person!
We are here by accident!

MATT/SAILOR: Can we stay for supper?

COACH/CYCLOPS: Sure!

(COACH picks up MATT's doll and bites its head, holding it in his mouth.)

MATT/SAILOR: That's not what I meant!

(COACH shakes the doll and drops it. MATT screams.)

MATT/SAILOR: Eeuw, I've been slimed!

(COACH tries to step on the dolls as he says…)

COACH/CYCLOPS:
My name is Polyphemus and my father is Poseidon.
If you try to hurt me he will give you quite a hidin'.

PROFESSOR/ODYSSEUS: My name is Nobody, good sir.

(MATT goes "psst!" and holds out a tiny wine bottle.)

PROFESSOR/ODYSSEUS: Hey, how 'bout a little wine?

(COACH takes it from MATT and drinks.)

COACH/CYCLOPS:
Nobody's a funny name. Is it Greek or Byzantine?

PROFESSOR/ODYSSEUS:
Nobody's Italian, sir. Please, just keep on drinking

COACH/CYCLOPS: Say, this wine's delicious! *(Stiffening)*
Uh-oh. What was I thinking?

(He falls over unconscious, bouncing on the stage and making the little dolls bounce in reaction. PROFESSOR and MATT walk the dolls over to the unconscious CYCLOPS. They stand on either side of his head, looking into his ears.)

MATT/SAILOR: Hey, Odysseus! I can see you!

(The illusion is that COACH's head is empty. MATT's doll sneezes into COACH's ear and the PROFESSOR's doll flips over, as if the sneeze went into one ear and out the other.)

MATT/SAILOR: Sorry!

(The dolls start climbing up COACH toward his head. First, they climb over COACH's foot…)

PROFESSOR/ODYSSEUS: Come on, hurry. Climb up the big hill.

MATT/SAILOR: Whee!

(...then over COACH's *knee...)*

PROFESSOR/ODYSSEUS: Climb over the medium hill.

MATT/SAILOR: Whee!

(...then they trip over COACH's *crotch.)*

PROFESSOR/ODYSSEUS: Uh-oh, tripped over a mole hill.

MATT/SAILOR: Eww!

*(*MATT *hands* PROFESSOR *a pencil, which* PROFESSOR *uses as a spear.)*

PROFESSOR/ODYSSEUS: Now's our chance, it's time to
    put my secret plan to work
This will get us out of here or my name's not Captain
    Kirk!

MATT/SAILOR: Stop it!

PROFESSOR/ODYSSEUS: I mean, Odysseus. Hi, ya!

*(*PROFESSOR *makes the doll stab the pencil into* COACH's *fake eye.)*

COACH/CYCLOPS: *(Grabbing the pencil)* Ow, I'm being killed!! I must remove this spear!

(The hand holding the pencil has some ripped red fabric hidden in it. COACH *dangles the fabric from his hand, creating the illusion of blood pouring out of the eye.)*

PROFESSOR/ODYSSEUS: Quick, let's get back to the ship. Let's haul ass outa here!

*(*COACH, *blinded, feels around, trying to find the dolls.)*

COACH/CYCLOPS: Marco?

MATT/SAILOR: Polo!

(The CYCLOPS *moves toward the voice, but the doll moves out of the way.)*

COACH/CYCLOPS: I swear I'll get you! Come back, Nobody, I will kill you!

PROFESSOR/ODYSSEUS: Ha! My name's Odysseus, not Nobody!

MATT/SAILOR: Shut up, will you?!

(Following the voices, COACH *leaps and lands between the two dolls, "launching" them in opposite directions.* MATT'*s doll sails into the audience. If the audience doesn't throw it back immediately,* MATT *says:)*

MATT/SAILOR: Little help, please!

(Someone will always toss the doll back onstage. MATT *picks it up.)*

PROFESSOR/ODYSSEUS: Hey, let me try!

*(*PROFESSOR *throws* his *doll into the audience. He makes a circle with his arms, like a basketball hoop. The audience member will invariably miss. In fact, it's better if they do.)*

COACH/CYCLOPS: What the hell. Throw me, throw me!

(He charges to the edge of the stage but stops short. The audience screams as they think that he is going to jump into the crowd.)

COACH/CYCLOPS: Marco?

PROFESSOR/ODYSSEUS: Polo!

*(*COACH/CYCLOPS *follows the voice and runs off screaming.)*

PROFESSOR/ODYSSEUS: Quick! He's gone! Let's run away. We really should be going.

MATT/SAILOR: *(Pointing to the audience)* No, I think we should stay here so they can practice throwing! *(He exits.)*

PROFESSOR/ODYSSEUS: The ocean made us want to quit
and throw in all the towels,
But we landed in Aeaea *(EE-EE-uh)*, The Land Of Only
Vowels.
We met the goddess Circe, and though I love the ladies
I knew she'd show no mercy, so we escaped to Hades!

(Spooky sounds. Light change.)

PROFESSOR/ODYSSEUS: Here in the underworld you
have to keep your head,
Because there's no escaping from the mean, ungrateful
dead!

*(MATT leaps on dressed as Jerry Garcia, with long grey hair
and beard, wearing a tie-dyed T-shirt. He has an arrow
stuck through his heel. Then COACH enters as KING
AGAMEMNON, with vampire teeth, crown, and cape.)*

PROFESSOR/ODYSSEUS:
Agamemnon! Achilles! Why do you two now appear?

MATT/ACHILLES: We're dead, you moron.

COACH/AGAMEMNON: *(A la Bela Lugosi)* Whaddaya
think, we like it here?

MATT/ACHILLES: I knew the thrill of victory in life,
I could not be beat!
But because of my heel I now know the agony of
defeat.

(The audience groans. The teachers glare at them.)

MATT/ACHILLES: Well, welcome to Hell!

MATT/COACH: *(Trying to scare the audience)* Wooo!

PROFESSOR/ODYSSEUS: I'm sad you're dead but I'm sure
you died with glory!

MATT/ACHILLES: Glory?! Are you crazy? Let me tell
you a little story.

(MATT and COACH throw PROFESSOR to the floor.)

MATT/ACHILLES: There's no honor dying for your country, blindly unawares.

COACH/AGAMEMNON: The honor comes from making other bastards die for theirs!

MATT/ACHILLES: If someone wants your sacrifice, do not volunteer.

BOTH: You'd rather be a slave on Earth than emperor down here.

(The two ghosts leave. Just before they vanish, COACH says—)

COACH/AGAMEMNON: Trick or treat! Whee!

PROFESSOR/ODYSSEUS: I must get home! I mustn't let these spirits so distract me
And note to self: I mustn't let the other two out-act me
(Rowing overdramatically)
We sailed away, facing monsters that were killa.
The worst was that dreaded six-headed monster Scylla!

(MATT and COACH stick their heads and hands into the doorway. They wear headbands with floppy dog ears attached to them and they each have dog puppets on both hands. The effect is six dog heads sticking through the door.)

MATT/COACH/SCYLLA: Bark! Bark! Bark!

COACH: Sa-right?

MATT: Sa-right!

COACH: So long!

MATT: By-bye!

COACH: *(As he disappears from the doorway)* Whee!

PROFESSOR/ODYSSEUS: We made it past the sirens.

(MATT and COACH re-enter with fire hats and sirens. They probably have not had time to remove their SCYLLA stuff. They circle and exit.)

PROFESSOR/ODYSSEUS: Yeah, that was pretty dumb.
Then we stumbled on to the sacred cattle of the sun!
We were warned not to touch the cattle no way, no how
But we really wanted burgers, and this was one mad
   cow!

(COACH *enters wearing the horse head. Cow horns have been*
attached lamely to it. He gruffly says, "Moo!", gives the
"Up yours" gesture, and exits.)

PROFESSOR/ODYSSEUS: At last I'm home. And I can
   finally have my life back.

(MATT *and* COACH *enter as the suitors. They hold heart*
shaped boxes of candy.)

COACH/MATT/SUITORS: Telemachus, is your mom
home?

PROFESSOR/ODYSSEUS: But I must kill these suitors so I
   can have my wife back!

(*Big fight scene.* ODYSSEUS *kills all the suitors [all portrayed*
by MATT *and* COACH*] with his bow and "arrows." In fact,*
ODYSSEUS *grabs a small bow from behind the bookcase, but*
no arrows. To shoot, he pulls back the string of the bow and
then releases it. The suitors hold small half-arrows, out of
view of the audience. When they get "shot" by ODYSSEUS,
they quickly hold the half-arrows up against their torsos.
It appears that the arrow is sticking into them, with the quill
end sticking out.)

(ODYSSEUS *shoots* MATT *and then misses* COACH.
Throughout the fight, suitors exit out the doorways after
they have been shot. ODYSSEUS *then shoots at another suitor*
*[*MATT*] who bats the invisible "arrow" away with his sword.*
The invisible "arrow" flies through the air and hits COACH
in the head as he enters through the doorway. He screams in
pain and exits.)

(ODYSSEUS *shoots twice more at* MATT, *who with his sword*
bats the "arrow" away both times. Then ODYSSEUS *shoots*

two "arrows" at MATT. MATT *bats them away, one after the
other, and the two arrows hit* COACH *in rapid succession as
he enters. He screams in pain and exits.)*

(Now ODYSSEUS *takes aim and shoots again at* MATT.
MATT *dodges the arrow by bending over backwards in slow
motion, a la* The Matrix. *The invisible arrow "flies" into the
audience. Now back at normal speed,* PROFESSOR *shoves*
MATT *out of the way and goes to retrieve the arrow from
under the chair of an audience member.* MATT *exits.*
PROFESSOR *ad-libs apologies as he quickly makes his way
back to the stage. When he arrives, he lifts up the arrow,
revealing it has a large woman's bra hanging from it.
He looks shocked, but he mimes putting a phone to his ear
and mouths "Call me".)*

PROFESSOR/ODYSSEUS: Watch this!

*(He "shoots" an arrow toward the stage left wall, then
watches it ricochet off the walls three times. After the third
ricochet, the single arrow runs through the two suitors—
who have entered screaming and with swords drawn—
pinning them together. This illusion is created by one of the
actors holding a half-arrow against his stomach with a quill
showing and the other actor holding a half-arrow against his
back with the arrow head showing. They shuffle off stage,
still pinned together by the arrow.* PROFESSOR *claps his
hands together several times as if to get the dirt off them.)*

PROFESSOR/ODYSSEUS: Revenge is sweet, but sweeter
    still's the sight of my old home.

*(*MATT/TELEMACHUS *skips on.)*

MATT/TELEMACHUS: Hi, Dad!

PROFESSOR/ODYSSEUS: Telemachus! My young son!
    Look at how you have grown!

MATT/TELEMACHUS: For twenty years, I've kept mom
    safe, and our home well-defended.

PROFESSOR/ODYSSEUS: But by your voice it sounds as
  though your testes aren't descended.
And where is she, my delicate young rose, Penelope?

(COACH *enters as* PENELOPE, *with ugly wig and skirt.*
He scratches his crotch.)

COACH/PENELOPE: Here I am, Odysseus! Your little
  chickadee!

PROFESSOR/ODYSSEUS: You haven't changed a bit,
  my love, and my poor heart is cheered.
You both look great. And look, you both have a little
  beard.

(PROFESSOR *feels* COACH'*s stubble.* COACH *slaps the hand*
away.)

COACH/PENELOPE: Knock it off!

MATT/TELEMACHUS: But gee wiz, dear Father,
what are we forgetting?

PROFESSOR/ODYSSEUS: Let's renew our vows—

COACH/PENELOPE: And have a great big fat Greek
  wedding!

(*They step down into their three specials before applause can*
start.)

PROFESSOR/CHORUS: Thus Odysseus made it home,
  despite how long it took

(COACH *attempts to interrupt, but* PROFESSOR *continues.*)

PROFESSOR/CHORUS: Yes, it took awhile, but it's shorter
  than the book.

COACH/CHORUS: The lesson here is perseverance,
  please make sure you heed it.

MATT/CHORUS: *The Idioddity's* over....

ALL THREE: ...and you didn't have to read it.

(They bow. Blackout. The bell rings and lights come back up. COACH *looks at his stopwatch.)*

COACH: Alright, class, that bell means it's the end of the first half and time for your midterm examination. Matthew, please distribute the papers.

*(*MATT *tosses a stack of midterm papers out into the audience. They float down over the crowd.)*

COACH: Keep one for yourself, pass the rest along to your neighbors. We also have some very sharp number two pencils for you to write...

*(*MATT *runs downstage with a big bunch of yellow pencils he's going to throw at the audience.* PROFESSOR *stops him.)*

COACH: Matt! No, no! Hand them out or leave them on the edge of the stage. Now, the midterm question you all need to give a written answer to is, "What are the two greatest books ever written and why?"

PROFESSOR: We'd like you to write a detailed answer, supported with citations and footnotes. There are extra pencils and midterms right down here. Please sign your name and leave your completed midterms here in a nice neat pile at the edge of the stage.

COACH: We'll begin the second half of the course with what is generally considered the greatest novel of the twentieth century—*Ulysses* by James Joyce. If you have not yet read the book, please do so during this fifteen minute break. Which begins—now!

*(*COACH *clicks his stopwatch, blows his whistle and moves his arm in a circle, like a football referee starting the clock. Blackout)*

END OF ACT ONE

ACT TWO

(The house lights fade out. The intermission music then fades as the stage lights fade to black.)

(Irish diddly-diddly music begins. A spot rises on COACH *as* STEPHEN DEDALUS, *wearing a flat-cap and wool sweater, and his athletic shorts.)*

COACH/STEPHEN: *(In an Irish accent)* The name is Stephen Dedalus. I'm on me way to the newspaper to deliver a letter from me boss. But I'm dawdlin' here on the strand. And I've been feelin' a bit guilty. On her deathbed me mother asked me to pray for her and I refused on principle. I'm an atheist, ya' see. And I'm estranged from me father.

(Spot fades on COACH *and rises on* PROFESSOR *as* LEOPOLD BLOOM, *holding a can of Guinness. He wears a cap and somewhat worn suit coat.)*

PROFESSOR/BLOOM: *(In an Irish accent)* I'm Leopold Bloom. I'm in advertisin'. I'm on me way to the newspaper to secure some advertisin' space. Me wife Molly Bloom and I haven't had marital relations in over eleven years, since the death of our infant son shortly after birth.

(If the audience laughs after "eleven years," PROFESSOR *can skip the rest of the line and say, "Think that's funny, do ya?" He drinks from the Guinness and freezes. Spot fades on* PROFESSOR *and rises on* MATT *as* MOLLY BLOOM, *wearing a bad wig and skirt.)*

MATT/MOLLY: *(In an American accent)* I'm Molly Bloom, Leopold Bloom's wife. I talk like an American because my Irish accent's crap. I'm about to undertake a concert tour under the management of Blazes Boylan. We're having an affair.

(He winks as the spot light cross fades to COACH. *Then* COACH's *recorded voice comes over the loudspeaker.* COACH's *lips don't move.)*

COACH: *(V O) Wow! The book Ulysses was ground-breaking on so many levels. It's not so much about the physical actions of the characters, but about their interior lives, their thoughts and motivations. And I love Joyce's use of inner monologue.*

(Cross fade to PROFESSOR, *who speaks out loud as* BLOOM.*)*

PROFESSOR/BLOOM: It's June sixteenth, nineteen hundred and four. Stephen Dedalus and I are wanderin' around Dublin. I'm a bit of a father figure to Stephen. Though because of my Jewishness, I'm an outsider in me own land.

(The audience doesn't react the way he expects. He stares at them and his thoughts come over the sound system. Your sound operator will need to be able to pause the recording to ride out laughs at various points in the rest of the scene. Fairly consistent laughs are marked with an asterisk [*])

PROFESSOR/BLOOM: *(V O) I hate this audience.* Look at all those blank stares. These people have no idea what Ulysses is about.*

(The lights fade up on each person as he speaks, and then dim as they finish.)

COACH: *(V O) This audience has no idea what Ulysses is about.*

MATT: *(V O) I have no idea what Ulysses is about.**

PROFESSOR: *(V O) What's everybody laughing at?* I hate *this audience.*

MATT: *(V O) I wonder if the audience has figured out that we haven't read any of these books?*

COACH: *(V O) Does this costume make me look fat?*

(PROFESSOR *and* MATT *shake their heads in the negative, but we hear their actual thoughts which are...)*

PROFESSOR: *(V O) Yeah.*

MATT: *(V O) Of course it does.*

PROFESSOR: *(V O) Like the south end of a horse going north...*

COACH: *(V O) Hey wait a minute! How did you hear my inner monologue?*

PROFESSOR: *(V O) Uh oh! I think our thoughts are being broadcast over the sound system. (Smiling at the audience) I love this audience!*

MATT: *(V O) Hey Coach, I don't have an inner monologue.*

COACH: *(V O) Really? Then what do I hear every time you have a thought?*

(MATT *looks up, listening. We hear crickets chirp three times.)*

COACH: *(V O) Now go ahead and finish up* Ulysses.

(COACH *and* PROFESSOR *start to exit.* MATT *stands in the center spotlight.)*

MATT: *(V O) What am I supposed to do?*

COACH: *(V O) Just do the Molly Bloom speech at the very end of the book. It's her great life affirming, stream of consciousness inner monologue.*

MATT: *(V O) I can't. I'm telling you, I don't have an inner monologue.*

PROFESSOR: *(V O) I'll do it. Gimme that.*

(He takes the wig and puts it on. COACH *and* MATT *exit.)*

PROFESSOR: *(V O) Here goes.*

(We now hear a female Irish voice.)

MOLLY BLOOM: *(V O) Then he held me under the Spanish Arch and I thought, why not him as anyone else and then I looked into his eyes and he asked me again yes and wondered if I would yes my...*

*(*PROFESSOR *has slowly become aware that this is not his voice. He looks around discreetly for the source of it, then:)*

PROFESSOR: *(V O) Wait a minute...whose inner monologue is this?*

MOLLY BLOOM: *(V O) Yours.*

PROFESSOR: *(V O. Confused) Why doesn't it sound like me?*

MOLLY BLOOM: *(V O) I don't know.*

PROFESSOR: *(V O. In a panic) Am I schizophrenic?*

MOLLY BLOOM: *(V O) I don't know!*

*(*PROFESSOR *mouths "Oh my God," grabs his head with both hands and bends over as if in pain. The female voice draws his attention up again.)*

MOLLY BLOOM: *(V O) ...and he asked again yes and wondered if I would yes my meadow blossom and then I held him in my arms yes and pulled him close to me against my...*

PROFESSOR: *(V O) I'm sorry to interrupt, but I must say you have a lovely voice.*

MOLLY BLOOM: *(V O) Thank you. And pulled him close to me...*

PROFESSOR: *(V O) What are you wearing?**

MOLLY BLOOM: *(V O) Nothing.*

PROFESSOR: *(V O) Really?*

MOLLY BLOOM: *(V O) I'm an inner monologue!*

PROFESSOR: *(V O) Right! Right. I'm sorry. My mistake. Please, continue.*

MOLLY BLOOM: *(V O) I held him in my arms yes and pulled him close to me against my...*

PROFESSOR: *(V O) I'm sorry to interrupt, again, but this is kind of the big climax to* Ulysses. *Would you mind if I took over my own inner monologue?*

MOLLY BLOOM: *(V O) It should be a woman.*

PROFESSOR: *(V O) Aw, please? As a favor from one inner monologue to another?*

MOLLY BLOOM: *(V O) Okay. Fine.*

PROFESSOR: *(V O) Great.*

MOLLY BLOOM: *(V O. Sotto voce) Stupid eedjit.*

(PROFESSOR *looks up—what did you say?—then moves on.*)

PROFESSOR: *(V O) Okay, let's see...and then I held him in my arms yes and pulled him close to me against my bosom... (He slows down during this, getting a little uncomfortable.) You know what? You were right. It should be a woman. Why don't you go ahead and finish this up? (Pause) Hello?*

MOLLY BLOOM: *(V O) No. I've had it. Finish the damn thing yourself.*

PROFESSOR: *(V O) But you were right, it should be a woman.*

MOLLY BLOOM: *(V O) Finish it yourself. Goodbye!*

(*We hear footsteps walking away.*)

PROFESSOR: *(V O) Wait! Come back!*

MOLLY BLOOM: *(V O) Good-bye!*

(*A door slams.* PROFESSOR *is puzzled how a voice can leave rooms and slam doors, but decides to move on.*)

PROFESSOR: *(V O) Forget it. Here goes. (Simply) And then I held him in my arms yes and pulled him close to me against*

*my bosom all perfume and his chest was pounding and yes I
told him yes I would yes...*

(On the final "yes", he bows as the lights fade to black.)

(Lights up. MATT *is onstage collecting the midterms from the
edge of the stage [where the audience has left them during
intermission]. He hands some to* COACH *and* PROFESSOR.*)*

*(Incidentally, there should be twenty-eight books left on stage
at intermission. The rest have been carried up to the bookshelf
during* ACT ONE. *If you put one more book onstage during
the intermission [we suggest a book that actually opens,
that you can use for* Anna Kareninakova], *you will have
twenty-nine. The, when you finish the "one sentence book
review" at the end of the show, all the books should have been
picked up.)*

COACH: All right, that was *Ulysses* by James Joyce.
But now it's time to grade your midterms. And I'm sure
we got some wonderful answers to our question, "What
are the two greatest books ever written and why?"

PROFESSOR: Here's an interesting answer. Steve
McDonald...? *(He looks around to see if Steve will identify
himself. He reads.)* Steve McDonald says, "The greatest
book ever written is the dictionary. It contains every
word, so in a sense it contains every book ever written."
All right, I'll give you that.

MATT: Here's a good one. Susie Epperson writes,
(Reading) "Green Eggs and Ham, I enjoy the rhyming."
I agree! "I do not lie there in the grass/I will not take it
up the—"

PROFESSOR & COACH: Matt!

MATT: *(Grading the answer)* A.

COACH: Mark Monforti says, "The greatest book ever
written is *Moby Dick*. Ha, ha, ha. I just made you say,
"Dick"." Okay, if that's the way it's going to be,
that's the way it's going to be! *(He storms off.)*

PROFESSOR: Coach, come back.

MATT: Aw, let him go, his jock strap's too tight.

PROFESSOR: Wow, listen to this.
Robin Selinger—Robin?—says... *(Reading)* "The greatest
book ever written is *Pat the Bunny*. This story combines
magic realism with a sensual tactile experience sure to
provide a *frisson* of pleasure to even the most jaded of
readers. The indeterminate gender of the bunny adds
to the mystery of this classic tale, and calls into question
our assumptions about traditional family values."
(He looks at the class, amazed) What are you doing in
the remedial class?

*(COACH enters dressed as AHAB, wearing a head scarf
He hops on one leg.)*

COACH/AHAB: The whale! Have you seen the Great
White Whale?

PROFESSOR: What are you doing?

COACH/AHAB: They want Dick? I'll give 'em Dick!

MATT: Hey!

PROFESSOR: Coach, we're doing the midterms now.
Stop hopping!

COACH/AHAB: *(Stopping)* Don't give me that! I control
men by my sheer force of will. *(He grimaces as though
trying to communicate telepathically.)*

PROFESSOR: Now what are you doing?

COACH/AHAB: I'm controlling you by my sheer force of
will! *(He grimaces again.)*

PROFESSOR: You look like you're having an accident.

(PROFESSOR exits. COACH stops grimacing.)

COACH/AHAB: I hate it when you ignore my sheer force
of will! *(He starts hopping again.)*

MATT: Coach, I've got your sheer force of will, but I don't understand why you're hopping.

COACH/AHAB: The whale took my leg. I must take his life. I need to board the *Pequod* and head for the open sea. I need the wind at me back, the sea in me face!

(PROFESSOR *runs on and tosses a bucket of water in* COACH's *face.*)

MATT: Hey!

COACH: What did you do that for?!

PROFESSOR: I was adding some realism.

COACH: Forget it!

(COACH *storms off.*)

MATT: No, you weren't. You threw water in his face.

PROFESSOR: Matthew, in the theater we call that "yes-anding".

MATT: Yeah, well in the real world we call it "censor-shipping"! This is how book banning starts. You were intimidating him.

PROFESSOR: Wait—throwing water is intimidation?

MATT: Of course.

PROFESSOR: Right, I remember when Stalin threw water on the peasants. What the hell are you—?

MATT: Oh cute. You demean what I say by making fun of it. That's a form a censorship. Do you realize they're now banning books like *Diary of Anne Frank* and *Of Mice and Men*?

PROFESSOR: Who are?

MATT: School Boards across the country, that's who are.

PROFESSOR: That's not true!

MATT: It is true! Students, we need to mount a national campaign to put these books back on the shelves. Are you with me? 'Cause if people...

(The crowd cheers. If they don't, PROFESSOR changes the following line to, "First of all, it doesn't sound like anybody's with you. And secondly, the books you're talking about are available everywhere." In any event, PROFESSOR interrupts MATT, and if the crowd makes noise says:)

PROFESSOR: Matthew, before you and your friends mount anything you should know the books you're talking about are available everywhere.

MATT: Right, pretty soon they're gonna start banning some really important books, like the manual to my Sony Play Station.

PROFESSOR: You know what, Matt? You're absolutely right. It's a *Brave New World*. *(He grabs MATT's midterms away from him.)*

MATT: Stop doing that! This is just like when John Lennon said The Beatles were more popular than Jesus. Everybody freaked out and started burning their Beatles records. And now, computer companies are telling you to burn C Ds! That's right, "Burn your own C Ds! Music is evil!"

PROFESSOR: Matthew! Burning C Ds is a good thing!

MATT: Oh-h-h! I knew you'd say something like that! You are just like those religious freaks who are banning *Harry Potter* because it promotes witchcraft. Now you can't find *Harry Potter* books, the movie, or the merchandise anywhere!

PROFESSOR: Sure you can. Matthew, I am just as against book banning as you are.

MATT: Right. You're not getting into my head, Nurse Ratchet.

PROFESSOR: *(As* MATT *covers his ears and sings or makes noises or screams)* Books should not be banned. No art should be...

(They argue strongly. COACH *enters and blows his whistle.)*

COACH: Look, you two are never going to agree, so we're just going to move on to those three great British authors.

PROFESSOR: Fine!

MATT: Great, I'll get the books together—

*(*MATT *looks for the books in the pile.* PROFESSOR *starts to go but stops.)*

COACH: By the way, Matt, did you ever get to the bottom of that sneezing business?

MATT: Yeah, actually Coach, I have....

COACH: Good.

MATT: It's pretty funny, I have a little confession to make....

COACH: I am going to kick this guy's ass!

MATT: Really?

COACH: Who is it?

MATT: Him! *(He points to a man in the audience.)*

COACH: Oh, really? A comedian right here in the front... *(Or second, or third, or whatever)* ...row!

*(*COACH *makes his way down to the guy.* MATT *and* PROFESSOR *take focus.)*

PROFESSOR: Wait, what happened?

MATT: Oh yeah! "Whenever Coach says Plato, everybody sneeze!" Sorry, man...

PROFESSOR: So he's the ringleader?

MATT: No, it was me. C'mere...

PROFESSOR: What?

COACH: What's your name? *(The audience member tells him)* _____ *(Name of audience member)* ...ladies and gentlemen!

(As the audience applauds, COACH asks the audience member to help out and gets his permission. They come onstage as MATT and PROFESSOR exit.)

COACH: Well, I don't appreciate your shenanigans. I'm going to have to make an example of you in front of the entire class. You just stand right about here. *(He looks toward the ceiling above the volunteer's head)* Great. I'll let you know when I need you. Right now, we're going to learn about three great British authors, their lives and their work. *(He now reads the introductions from note cards that he's pulled out of his pocket. There are nine cards, one for each author's introduction, and one for each of the six questions that follow.)* Our first author is an English woman who never married. Her books deal with middle class people and their daily routine. Her most famous novels are *Sense and Sensibility* and *Pride and Prejudice*. Please bang your hands together for Jane Austen!

(MATT enters, wearing a blonde wig and skirt.)

COACH: How are you doing, Jane?

MATT/J AUSTEN: No, Coach, how *you* doing?

COACH: Just fine. Author Number Two was a religious zealot until her twenties. She wrote under a man's name so that her work would be taken seriously and her best known books are *Silas Marner* and *Middlemarch*. Give it up for George Eliot!

(PROFESSOR enters, wearing a black wig and skirt. He has a blonde curly wig tucked into the back of the skirt so the audience can't see it.)

PROFESSOR/G ELIOT: Hi, Coach. Hi, Jane.

COACH: George, *(Audience guy's name)*. *(Audience guy's name)*, George.

PROFESSOR/G ELIOT: Hi, *(Audience member's name)*.

COACH: Author Number Three wrote *Orlando* and *To The Lighthouse,* and was a member of the Bloomsbury Group. After several nervous breakdowns, she drowned herself at age fifty-nine. But there's no reason to be afraid of Virginia Woolf!

(PROFESSOR holds out the blond wig to COACH, as if COACH will play Virginia Woolf. But COACH steps upstage and looks at the audience guy. PROFESSOR helps the guy put on the wig.)

COACH: *(Presenting)* Virginia Woolf!

PROFESSOR/G ELIOT: *(Presenting)* Peter Frampton! *(Or Roger Daltry or Twisted Sister or Christina Aguilera, whichever blond curly rocker your audience will recognize)*

COACH: Okay, let's learn about these authors. Jane Austen...

MATT/J AUSTEN: Yes?

COACH: Critics have noted that there isn't much action in your novels. How would you respond?

MATT/J AUSTEN: I think that's a terrible criticism. I've always written from my life experience, and stayed true to myself. And I think my success speaks for itself.

COACH: I think it speaks very loudly.

MATT/J AUSTEN: Thank you.

COACH: George Eliot...

PROFESSOR/G ELIOT: Yes?

COACH: You were one of the first psychological/ sociological novelists. Why were you drawn to this style?

PROFESSOR/G ELIOT: Interesting. You know, D H
Lawrence did say I was the first to put the action on
the inside. I've always felt that a person's interior life
and machinations were much more interesting than
exterior meanderings.

COACH: I completely agree. Bachelorette Number
Three, if I were a banana, how would you peel me?

*(If the guy doesn't say anything, COACH goes on to the next
line. But as often as not, the audience member will come up
with some sort of answer. Sometimes it's a little hard for
the audience to hear, so one of the cast members may need
to repeat it. In any case, if the volunteer says just about
anything in response to the question, it will get a big laugh.
The three guys get on their knees, bow down to him, then
get up.)*

COACH: Maybe I'll just stick to the cards. Bachelorette
Number One, it has been said that *Pride and Prejudice*
is a perceptive examination of the relationship between
classes in Britain. Do you have a problem with the class
system?

MATT/J AUSTEN: Yes, I do. I don't think the class
system works at all.

COACH: Really?

MATT/J AUSTEN: We've been here all night... *(Or "day",
if it's a matinee)* ...and this class hasn't learned a damn
thing!

COACH: Although I think... *(Name of volunteer)* ...is
learning a little lesson.

PROFESSOR: Don't sit in the front row.

(COACH moves on to the next card.)

COACH: Bachelorette Number Two, you claim to be
George Eliot, yet your given name is Mary Anne Evans.
Who are you really?

PROFESSOR/G ELIOT: I am both the Professor and Mary Anne! *(Giving the volunteer a little shove on the arm)* Beat that, Funny Boy!

COACH: Bachelorette Number Three, do you have a cold?

(The volunteer will usually say "No." To which COACH replies...)

COACH: Then why the hell are you sneezing in my class?!

(If the volunteer says, "Yes," the only difference is that COACH slightly changes the phrasing to say something like, "Is that why you're sneezing in my class?!")

MATT & PROFESSOR: Coach, calm down! Let it go. Etc.

COACH: Okay, I'll let it go. He's been playing along somewhat manfully. That concludes the questions. The moment of truth is at hand. I am going to go on a dream date with one of these three eligible bachelorettes.

(MATT and PROFESSOR hop up and down and clap in excited anticipation. During COACH's speech, PROFESSOR tells Virginia Woolf to hop with them. He usually does.)

COACH: By your applause, will it be Bachelorette Number One...?

(COACH gestures to MATT. The applause is always weak. MATT leaves in disgust.)

COACH: Bachelorette Number Two...?

(COACH gestures to PROFESSOR. Again the applause is weak. PROFESSOR goes to the bookcase and takes off his wig and skirt.)

COACH: Or by your applause will it be Bachelorette Number Three?

(The audience always votes overwhelmingly for Number Three. Catchy game show music plays. COACH puts his arm around him and whispers to the volunteer that he's doing great and to hang here for another minute. MATT reenters tossing confetti. He puts Hawaiian leis around the necks of COACH and the volunteer.)

(The music fades so PROFESSOR can speak over it.)

PROFESSOR: Congratulations! You lucky kids are going to enjoy a fun-filled romantic weekend getaway trip for two to beautiful... *(Insert the name of a very ugly nearby town or rundown local kitschy tourist trap or Notell Motel here. This can also be "...a romantic candle lit dinner for two at..." the least romantic eating establishment in town.)* Let's blow them a kiss goodbye!

(They blow a kiss at the audience.)

COACH: *(To volunteer)* Look right there.

(COACH points at MATT, who takes their picture with a Polaroid camera. PROFESSOR gets in the picture too. They hand the volunteer the photo and then help him offstage.

COACH: *[Audience member's name]*, ladies and gentlemen!

(COACH helps him back into the audience, telling him to watch his step.)

COACH: One more time... *(Name of volunteer)* ...everybody!

PROFESSOR: *(As the applause dies)* That's not fair. He doesn't have a script and he's funnier than we are.

(COACH picks up the huge copy of War and Peace *that's been on the floor since ACT ONE.)*

COACH: The only way to top that is *War and Peace*.

PROFESSOR: Woah! No!

MATT: We've already covered *War and Peace*!

COACH: Not to my satisfaction.

PROFESSOR: Coach, we still have all these books left to cover before graduation. *(Picking one up from the floor)* Let's just do something simple, like Dante's *Divine Comedy*.

COACH: Okay, only one thing you need to know about *The Divine Comedy*. Not funny. This genius wrote a comedy and left out the jokes. It's like Carrot Top. *(Or whoever is the least funny comedian that everyone has heard about).*

(COACH tosses the book upstage.)

MATT: Coach, why don't we cover that other novel by Tolstoy, you know, the one about the sexy Russian tennis player who throws herself under a train?

(COACH picks up a book from the floor and hands it to MATT.)

COACH: Anna Kareninakova?

MATT: Yeah! *(He opens the book and turns it lengthwise, like a centerfold. Then he carries it upstage and places it on the bookshelf.)*

COACH: Guys, don't be so afraid of *War and Peace*. *(To the audience)* If you take nothing else away from this course, take this: do not be intimidated by the great authors. They were regular guys. They put their pants on one leg at a time.

PROFESSOR: What about Emily Bronte?

COACH: She put her dress on one leg at a time.

MATT: Gertrude Stein?

COACH: Not sure.

PROFESSOR: Coach, I have a confession to make. I couldn't finish reading *War and Peace*.

MATT: Me, either.

COACH: *(To MATT)* How far did you get?

MATT: Title page.

COACH: Well, you're both pathetic. *(Handing* War and Peace *to* MATT*)* I finished it and it's fantastic. It's got everything: life and death, love and hate, war and peace. You name it, it's in here.

*(*MATT *has opened the huge book.* COACH *pulls out the* War and Peace Cliff Notes *tucked inside.* MATT *carries* War and Peace *up to the bookshelf.)*

PROFESSOR: Anybody can read the *Cliff Notes!* But I couldn't finish the real book. I'm not man enough.

COACH: Well, Matt is.

MATT: No, I'm not.

PROFESSOR: No, he's not!

COACH: You're not man enough?

(They argue briefly until COACH *blasts his whistle.)*

COACH: Take a knee, fellas.

(They kneel. Dramatic music plays. COACH *paces.)*

COACH: Where the hell did that music come from? I know you're scared. You feel like it's the bottom of the ninth, you're down by four, two outs and the bases are empty. Well, look at the bright side. At least you're not a season ticket holder for the Los Angeles Clippers *(Or your crappy local team)*. Tolstoy said that men are controlled by destiny. Well this our destiny, men. We did not choose *War and Peace*. *War and Peace* chose us. Look at these students. There they sit with bright tails and bushy eyes. These are some of the slowest minds in the developed world and they're counting on us. So let's get out there and tackle *War and Peace*. The longest novel in the history of Russia!

ALL: U S A! U S A! U S A! U S A! U S A!

(They run offstage. Epic music begins. MATT *enters, walking very formally, with a sign rolled up under his arm. He stops and reveals the sign which is written in Russian. In the original production the sign said, in Russian: "This is actual Russian. Are you impressed?" [See page 102] He then reveals the other side of the sign which reads, "*COACH *is making a very long costume change." He exits.)*

*(*COACH *enters wearing a military coat and a really bad wig. The audience laughs. He stares them down.)*

COACH/ANDREY: Page One. I am Andrey Bolkonsky. Against the background of Napoleon's impending invasion of Russia, I am attending a massive society party in Saint Petersburg, at which we meet all of the major characters of *War and Peace.*

*(*PROFESSOR *enters.)*

PROFESSOR/PIERRE: Page Five. I am Pierre... *(Coughing nastily)* ...Nastykhov. *(He, too, stares down the audience.)*

COACH/ANDREY: *(To* PIERRE*)* Page twenty-two. I am cynical and arrogant, at war with my father's outdated feudal values.

PROFESSOR/PIERRE: *(To* ANDREY*)* Page fifty-five. Despite my youth, I am thoughtful and optimistic— completely at peace with myself.

COACH/ANDREY: Wait! I'm at war...

PROFESSOR/PIERRE: ...and I'm at peace!

PROFESSOR/COACH: Two great tastes that taste great together!

(They laugh and embrace in the manly Russian style. MATT *enters as* NATASHA*, stepping between them.)*

MATT/NATASHA: Title page. I am Natasha Rostov—the embodiment of innocent feminine sexuality. Hello, boys!

COACH/ANDREY: Will you marry me?

MATT/NATASHA: Yes, Andre, of course.

PROFESSOR/PIERRE: But I am the fictional embodiment of Tolstoy himself.

MATT/NATASHA: It never hurts to sleep with the author.

(NATASHA *shoves* ANDREY *aside and exits with* PIERRE, *arm in arm.*)

COACH/ANDREY: Page eighty-seven. As the embodiment of Mother Russia, I join the army to fight at the front, seeking honor and glory.

(*We hear the sounds of battle.* COACH *mimes shooting a rifle.*)

COACH/ANDREY: Bang! Bang! Bang! (*He mimes being shot*) Great bowls of borscht! I'm shot.

(*We hear heavenly harps.*)

COACH/ANDREY: Wait! I'm having.... (*He lifts his wig off his head with both hands and then puts it back on—as if it briefly floated away from his head.*) ...an epiphany. And it is hair raising!

(*He exits.* PROFESSOR *shoves* MATT *on, protesting.*)

MATT: But, I don't—page...page...?

(MATT *obviously doesn't know what's next.* COACH *sticks his head out.*)

COACH: One thirty-five!

(COACH *tosses* MATT *the* Cliff Notes *and exits.*)

MATT: Page one thirty-five. Oh! Russian nicknames are explained. The suffix "Ovich" means "son of." Hence, Ivanovich, means "son of Ivan." Interesting.

(MATT *dashes off as* PROFESSOR *runs on.*)

PROFESSOR/PIERRE: Page one seventy-eight. I decide to assassinate Napoleon, that bitchovich.

(PROFESSOR *exits.* COACH *enters.*)

COACH/ANDREY: Page two eighty-five. My father receives word that I have died. *(Beat)* I know the feeling.

(COACH exits. PROFESSOR pulls MATT on. MATT's furiously leafing through the Cliff Notes.)

PROFESSOR: Page three oh four. Natasha Rostov decides she does not want to marry Boris! *(He exits.)*

MATT/NATASHA: *(Picking up his cue)* No, I don't want to marry Boris! Wait, who's Boris? Who's Boris?!

(He exits. COACH enters.)

COACH/ANDREY: Page three fifty-four. I'm not really dead, but I return home and scare my wife so badly that *she* dies.

(Trying to be helpful, MATT runs on, screams, throws his Cliff Notes in the air and drops dead. COACH shakes his head and exits. MATT leaps up, totally lost. He flips through the Cliff Notes trying to figure out what's next.)

MATT: Um, 1983. Mikhael Gorbachov spills ketchup on his forehead!

(MATT tosses the Cliff Notes in the air, then crosses upstage. COACH runs on.)

COACH/ANDREY: Page four oh four. Russia's transition from an agricultural to an industrial society is mirrored by my arrival at the family estate....

(MATT's now standing behind COACH. He snatches the wig off COACH's head.)

COACH/ANDREY: ...Bald Hills.

(COACH exits. MATT strokes the toupee.)

MATT/NATASHA: *(A la Gollum)* Precious. My precious.

(MATT exits as PROFESSOR runs on.)

PROFESSOR: Page four seventy-one. My assassination attempt fails. The war continues.

(We again hear the sounds of battle. MATT *runs on as* PROFESSOR *exits.)*

MATT: 1989, the Soviet Union falls.

*(*MATT *turns to try and pick up the study guide, but* PROFESSOR *runs on fast and knocks* MATT *down.* PROFESSOR *quickly makes sure* MATT's *okay, then says:)*

PROFESSOR: 2005 *(Or whatever year it is)*, Matthew falls.

MATT: Page four seventy-three. Why don't you open your eyes, Professor? I was standing right there! *(He exits.)*

PROFESSOR: *(Surprised)* Page four eighty-five. At least I know the difference between "invincible" and "invisible".

*(*MATT *runs back on.)*

MATT: Page four ninety-three. Stop censoring me and get off your high horse!

PROFESSOR: Oh, you wanna go there? Page four ninety-eight! Hell freezes over when you actually read one of the books we're trying to teach!

MATT: Well, I guess that brings us to page five hundred. What do you know? Bite me!

(He heaves the Cliff Notes *at* PROFESSOR, *who's caught off-guard.)*

PROFESSOR: Wha—how dare you?!

(Their argument escalates until COACH *enters and stops them with his whistle.)*

COACH: This is a war! Stop fighting!

PROFESSOR: Coach, we're wasting time on *War and Peace*. We should be covering all these books. *(He takes off his Russian peasant shirt as he speaks.)* And you know what? Tolstoy was wrong. We do have free will and I'm exercising mine right now!

(He throws his peasant shirt upstage, and starts to exit, but he stops as he hears MATT's *next point.)*

MATT: Look, I hate to agree with him, but Professor's right. What is your obsession with *War and Peace*? You know we still have to cover *The Grapes of Wrath*!

PROFESSOR: Yeah, and Sherlock Holmes!

MATT: *The Scarlet Letter!*

PROFESSOR: *The Three Musketeers!*

MATT: *(A la Bela Lugosi) Dracula!*

PROFESSOR: *Doctor Jekyll and Mister Hyde!*

COACH: Don't you understand? If we finish *War and Peace* we've covered all these books! It has the swordplay of *The Three Musketeers*, the infidelity of *The Scarlet Letter*, the mystery of Sherlock Holmes, and the inhumanity of *The Grapes of Wrath*.

*(*COACH *crosses toward the bookshelf.* PROFESSOR *follows him.)*

PROFESSOR: But we haven't finished reading *War and Peace*, so how can we go on?

*(*MATT *kneels and ties his shoe.)*

MATT: *(Innocently)* Well, you know what, Tolstoy said it himself. Don't over think. Be in the moment. Forget reason and strategy, and simply have faith in the human spirit. Live your life instinctively, with a passion for spontaneity.

*(*PROFESSOR *and* COACH *stare at* MATT, *who suddenly realizes they're looking at him.)*

MATT: Apparently somebody didn't read the title page.

COACH: Page eight hundred and seventy-seven. The climax of *War and Peace*, the battle of Borodino. Bring it in.

(COACH *puts out his hand, calling them over to huddle.*
MATT *and* PROFESSOR *put their hands on top of* COACH'*s.)*

ALL: One, two three - Tolstoy!

(They push their hands down—a huddle break. The 1812
Overture *begins.* MATT *[who's still holding* COACH'*s wig]*
tosses the wig up into the air. MATT *and* PROFESSOR *exit.*
COACH *catches the wig on his head.)*

COACH/ANDREY: Toss me my weapon!

*(*PROFESSOR *tosses* COACH *the stick horse.)*

COACH/ANDREY: Stand behind me, men! Napoleon
will take no prisoners! There is no such thing as polite
war! No magnanimity to the enemy...

*(*MATT *runs on and hits* COACH *with a soccer ball.*
[All the balls are in fact inflatable beach balls shaped
like various sports balls.])

MATT: Attack! Attack!

*(*MATT *hits* COACH *with a basketball and exits.)*

COACH/ANDREY: *(Improvising)* The French are firing
cannon balls!

*(*PROFESSOR *runs on from the other wing and hits* COACH
with a ball.)

COACH: What are you doing?!

PROFESSOR: We're controlled by destiny!

(He hits COACH *with another ball and exits.)*

COACH: Stop it!

*(*MATT *has entered with an entire bag of balls.)*

MATT: We can't! *(Chucking a ball at* COACH*)* We have not
chosen the balls. The balls have chosen us!

*(*MATT *fires another ball at* COACH, *then starts throwing*
balls to the audience.

COACH: This isn't in *War and Peace!*

(PROFESSOR has entered with a whole bag of balls. He throws one at COACH.)

PROFESSOR: *Au contraire, mon petite fromage! (Hitting him with another one)* You said *everything* is in *War and Peace* !

(PROFESSOR and MATT empty their ball sacks into the front row and encourage the class to chuck the balls at COACH.)

PROFESSOR & MATT: *(Varioius)* Attack! Attack! Throw those at Coach!

(They exit.)

(The audience throws the balls at COACH and he dodges/kicks/hits/throws/bats the balls away.)

COACH: Bring it on! Is that all you got? Whaddaya, play for the *(Local terrible team)*? *(Referring to audience member who has just thrown a ball at him.)* And you, sir, have got a lot of balls! *(Trying to get back on track)* I have abandoned my wife and children because I do not expect to live out this day. War is to the death, and I fully expect to die!

(MATT and PROFESSOR run back on dressed as musketeers. They carry long metal foils—in fact, MATT carries two. He wears Mickey Mouse ears and large white Mickey Mouse gloves. The audience laughs. COACH drops his stick horse and wig on the stage. MATT tries to act dignified but the audience keeps laughing. In frustration, with his silly glove, MATT gives the audience the finger.)

COACH/PROFESSOR: *(Various)* Hey! Knock it off!

(MATT tosses a sword to COACH.)

COACH: Who the hell are you?

MATT: The Three Mouseketeers!

PROFESSOR: Musketeers, dumb ass!

MATT: *(With great dignity)* It's pronounced *Dumas (Doo-MAH)*.

PROFESSOR: I am D'artagnan!

MATT: I am Annette Funicello

COACH/PROFESSOR: Stop it!

PROFESSOR: It's all for one!

MATT: And every man for himself! *En garde, monsieur!*

(COACH duels with PROFESSOR while MATT cowers. PROFESSOR waves his musketeer plume in COACH's face, and COACH bats it away. Finally, they get up close to each other, nose to nose. PROFESSOR rubs COACH's forehead.)

PROFESSOR: Look! I can see myself!

COACH: Really?

(COACH head butts PROFESSOR, who runs off holding his head. MATT tries to exit but COACH stops him.)

COACH: What part of France are you from?

MATT: Disneyland Paris! *(There is a brief bit of swordplay, with MATT ending up near the doorway. COACH throws him through one door and PROFESSOR flies on through the other, dressed as SHERLOCK HOLMES.)*

PROFESSOR/SHERLOCK: Quickly, Watson! The game's afoot!

COACH: *(Confused)* What the hell is going on?

(They start dueling.)

PROFESSOR/SHERLOCK: Elementary, my dear Coach!

(SHERLOCK parries COACH's sword attack with his pipe. The pipe breaks to SHERLOCK's chagrin and COACH's delight.)

PROFESSOR/SHERLOCK: Bollocks.

(They continue fighting)

PROFESSOR/SHERLOCK: Your assertion is that *War and Peace* contains the elements of all the great books. Do you deny it?!

COACH: I do not!

PROFESSOR/SHERLOCK: Ah-ha! Then you'll be overjoyed when Matthew and I illustrate the rest of *War and Peace* with our favorite characters from fiction!

(MATT *comes on dressed as* DRACULA, *with false teeth he can barely speak through.*)

MATT/DRACULA: I vant to drink your blahhd.

BOTH: What? What are you?

COACH: My *what*?

MATT/DRACULA: Blahhd! Blahhd!

COACH: Who are you!?

MATT/DRACULA: Your blood! Dracula? Bram Stoker? Never mind. I'm traveling to London, vere I vill...

(PROFESSOR *howls like a wolf.*)

MATT/DRACULA: Oh, no! It's Beowulf! (*He exits.*)

PROFESSOR/SHERLOCK: No, Watson. It's the Hound of the Baskervilles!

(MATT *runs on wearing a dog mask and howls again.* COACH *exits in disgust.* MATT *follows him.*)

(*The lights jump to the Walden special, with the previous Walden music. The* PROFESSOR *sits there, fishing like the first two Waldens. Then scary shark music is heard over the Walden music.*)

(PROFESSOR'*s pole jerks to the right, then to the left. He's then pulled sharply offstage, screaming.*)

(COACH *and* MATT *enter wearing long Z Z Top type beards.*)

COACH & MATT: The Brothers Karamozov!

*(They briefly juggle bean bags, finish flashily, ta-da and exit.
PROFESSOR runs on as DR HENRY JEKYLL, carrying an
Ehrlenmeyer flask full of blue liquid.)*

PROFESSOR/DR JEKYLL: The long Russian War is over.
Napoleon did surrender. What a marvelous party.
Pleasure to meet you. I am Doctor Henry Jekyll! *(He
drinks out of the Ehrlenmeyer flask.)* Hmm, tastes great!
(Suddenly MR HYDE*)* Less filling! Join me, friends!

*(MATT runs through as the HUNCHBACK OF NOTRE
DAME, ringing a hand bell.)*

MATT/HUNCHBACK: Sanctuary! Sanctuary! *(He exits.)*

PROFESSOR/MR HYDE: Ring the bell! Sound the alarm!

*(COACH lumbers through wearing a rubber FRANKENSEIN
mask. The face is cut out, so we see COACH's face but with
the monster's flat head.)*

COACH/FRANKENSTEIN: Uhh! Uhh!

PROFESSOR/MR HYDE: Go ravage Madeline Kahn!
I have found a way to unleash man's dark side!
Nothing can stop me now!

*(COACH has exited. MATT enters wearing a Wonder
Woman-type bustier with a large "T" on it. He confronts
MR HYDE.)*

MATT/TESS: Not so fast, monster. I am Tess! Tess of the
D'Urbervilles!

*(COACH re-enters as HESTER PRYNNE, wearing a bonnet
and an apron with the scarlet "A" on his chest.)*

COACH/HESTER: Leave us alone! We shall not be
shamed!

*(COACH curtsies. PROFESSOR looks at the letters on their
chests.)*

PROFESSOR/MR HYDE: Oh, no! They've discovered my
weakness! "T" and "A"!

(COACH *chases* PROFESSOR *off.*)

MATT/TESS: I am off! To the lighthouse, and beyond!

*(*MATT *exits.* PROFESSOR *hops in on one leg as a pirate.)*

PROFESSOR/LONG JOHN SILVER: Argh! Avast there, mateys. I need to feel the wind at me back, the sea in me face!

(COACH *runs on as* AHAB *and throws a bucket of water on* PROFESSOR. *Then he picks up his stick horse and begins to hop on one leg, too.)*

COACH/AHAB: I'm just trying to add a little realism! *I'm* Captain Ahab! Who do you think you are, ya lily-livered sea monkey?

PROFESSOR/LONG JOHN SILVER: I'm not Captain Ahab! I'm Long John Silver, ya sewage drinkin' bilge rat!

COACH/AHAB: *War and Peace* ain't big enough for two peg-legged caricatures!

PROFESSOR/LONG JOHN SILVER: Oh, yeah? What's a pirate's favorite letter?

COACH/AHAB: Arrr!

PROFESSOR/LONG JOHN SILVER: Arrr!

COACH/PROFESSOR: Oh! Aye! See! You! Pee!

(They have a short sword fight, PROFESSOR *with a plastic sword and* COACH *using the stick horse as a sword.)*

COACH: Wait a second! I'm putting my foot down!

(He does. Without COACH *being aware of it,* PROFESSOR *charges and impales himself on the stick horse.* COACH *pulls it out and* PROFESSOR *exits.)*

COACH: I've gotten off-track. I've got to finish *War and Peace* if it's the last thing I do! *(He picks up his toupee off the floor and slaps it on his head. He uses the stick horse as if it were a gun.)* On page one thousand, Tolstoy condemns the abuse of the lower classes!

(MATT *enters wearing a flat cap and holding a hobo stick.)*

MATT/TOM JOAD: Whenever there's a cop beating up a guy, I'll be there.

COACH: We are not doing *Grapes of Wrath!*

(COACH *clobbers* MATT *with the stick horse.)*

MATT/TOM JOAD: Reform the peasantry!

(COACH *hits him again.* MATT *runs off.)*

COACH: Page two thousand and two. Spirituality keeps men from becoming animals.

(PROFESSOR *runs on wearing a pig nose.)*

PROFESSOR: Two legs bad! Two legs bad!

COACH: *Animals!* Not *Animal Farm!*

(COACH *hits* PROFESSOR'S *pig nose, knocking it to the floor.* PROFESSOR *runs off as* MATT *runs on in an ape mask. He makes ape noises.)*

COACH: No *Origin of Species!*

(COACH *punches* MATT, *who exits.* PROFESSOR *returns blowing a conch shell.)*

COACH: Or *Lord of the Flies!*

(*He sends* PROFESSOR *off by elbowing him in the conch.* MATT *runs on wearing bobbling antennae on his head.)*

MATT: Look, I'm a cockroach! I'm a cockroach! Ha, ha, ha, ha!

(COACH *pushes* MATT *to the ground and steps on his bottom, squishing him.* MATT *makes squealing screaming sounds, then lays still.)*

COACH: No Kafka!

(MATT *gets up and runs off.)*

COACH: Page three thousand three hundred and thirty-three. Human behavior is irrational. It will always be a mystery!

(PROFESSOR *returns as* SHERLOCK HOLMES.)

PROFESSOR/SHERLOCK: Wrong again, Inspector Lestrade!

(COACH *tosses his wig at the* PROFESSOR. *The toupee "attacks"* PROFESSOR's *throat. He runs off, screaming.*)

COACH: Page ten thousand two hundred and sixteen. The Russian bourgeoise fear that by empowering the lower classes, they will rise up like monsters and kill their former masters.

(MATT *returns, dressed and acting like* FRANKENSTEIN.)

COACH: What are you doing?

(MATT *tosses the headpiece to the floor.*)

MATT: *(Pouting as he exits)* You said, "Monsters..."

COACH: Page twenty-two thousand eight hundred and eleven. *War and Peace* is both the story of a nation and the story of individuals, like a combination of *The Aeneid* and *The Iliad*.

(MATT *runs on as* ACHILLES *in armor and holding a spear, but also with a bandaged-wrapped head and dark glasses like The Invisible Man.*)

MATT/ACHILLES: I'm Achilles and I am invisible!

(*He stabs* COACH *with his spear. The* PROFESSOR *returns as* ODYSSEUS *and does his William Shatner impression.*)

PROFESSOR/ODYSSEUS: Beam me up, Scotty. This story sucks!

(*He stabs* COACH *with his sword.*)

COACH: We're not doing Ralph Ellison, H G Wells, or William Shatner!

(COACH *grabs* MATT *by the collar and throws him at* PROFESSOR. *They run each other through with their weapons and collapse to the floor.*)

MATT/ACHILLES: *(As he dies)* How did he see me...?

PROFESSOR/ODYSSEUS: I'm dead, Jim!

(He dies. COACH *struggles, dying.)*

COACH: Finally, page one million nine hundred and seventy-six thousand two hundred and twenty-five second paragraph, two-thirds of the way down the page. On his death bed, Andrey comes to understand that life and death, love and hate, war and peace are not opposites. They are unities. An idea first expressed by that great Greek philosopher, Plato!

(The class sneezes, triggering hundreds of inflatable balls to drop from overhead. COACH *falls dead. Blackout)*

(The school bell rings. Lights up)

(COACH *clicks off his stopwatch then high fives* MATT *and the* PROFESSOR. COACH *applauds the class while* PROFESSOR *bows grandly.)*

PROFESSOR: Thank you, ladies and gentlemen. Thank you so much.

(But MATT *stops them.)*

MATT: Wait a minute, we aren't finished. I know you all want to get out of here, but we still have all these books left to cover.

PROFESSOR: Woah, no!

COACH: Weren't you listening? We did *War and Peace.* We're finished.

MATT: Give us about twenty-five more minutes...

*(MATT *exits.)*

PROFESSOR: Pay no attention to The Idiot. I just want to thank you all for coming and let you know that...

(But MATT *returns wearing a high pointed wizard's hat and long beard.)*

MATT: Join me hobbits! We must battle....

*(*PROFESSOR *and* COACH *just stare at him.)*

MATT: Coach, they need to graduate! We haven't even done a review.

COACH: We can't. We're out of time.

MATT: Okay, give me two minutes. I can encapsulate each of these great books in a single sentence.

PROFESSOR: No you can't!

MATT: Try me. *(He takes off his Hawaiian shirt and throws it to the floor.)*

PROFESSOR: Okay. Um...*The Origin of Species.*

MATT: We came from apes!

*(*PROFESSOR *and* COACH *react, surprised.)*

COACH: *Interpretation of Dreams.*

MATT: I love my mother.

COACH: That's it?

MATT: No, I *really* love my mother.

*(*PROFESSOR *grabs a book from the floor.)*

PROFESSOR: Okay, the *Tao.*

MATT: It was down three hundred points for the week, but I don't...

PROFESSOR: No, not the Dow, the *Tao.*

(He tosses the book to MATT.*)*

MATT: Oh, the *Tao.* Desire nothing.

COACH: *Walden.*

MATT: Simplify your life.

PROFESSOR: *Thus Spake Zarathustra.*

MATT: God is dead.

COACH: *1984.*

MATT: Don't trust the government.

PROFESSOR: *Animal Farm.*

MATT: Don't trust the pigs.

COACH: *The Feminine Mystique.*

MATT: Don't trust—the pigs.

(PROFESSOR *and* COACH *now begin to pick up books from the floor and toss them to* MATT *as they say the title. They don't toss books that have already been picked up and placed on the up-center bookshelf during the course of the show. They also don't toss books when they say movie titles. By the time the scene is finished, there should be no more books left on the floor.)*

PROFESSOR: *(Tossing a book) Silent Spring.*

MATT: Don't trust big business.

COACH: *(Tossing a book) Canterbury Tales.*

MATT: Don't take a long trip with people who like to tell long boring stories. *(He catches each book and stacks them in his arms.)*

PROFESSOR: *(Tossing a book) Alice in Wonderland.*

MATT: Don't do drugs.

COACH: *(Tossing a book) On the Road.*

MATT: Do drugs.

PROFESSOR: *(Tossing a book) Frankenstein.*

MATT: Don't mess with nature.

COACH: *The Odyssey.*

MATT: Don't write a book in Greek that nobody can understand.

PROFESSOR: *(Tossing a book) Ulysses.*

MATT: Don't write a book in English that nobody can understand.

COACH: *(Tossing a book) Heart of Darkness.*

MATT: He dies in the end.

PROFESSOR: *Camille.*

MATT: She dies at the end.

COACH: *Sunset Boulevard.*

MATT: Dies at the beginning.

PROFESSOR: *The Bible.*

MATT: Comes back to life at the end.

COACH: *(Tossing a book) The Great Gatsby.*

MATT: Rich people are screwed up.

PROFESSOR: *(Tossing a book) Das Capital.*

MATT: The workers are screwed.

COACH: *Oliver Twist.*

MATT: The workers are screwed.

PROFESSOR: *(Tossing a book) To Kill A Mockingbird.*

MATT: The mockingbirds are screwed!

COACH: *(Tossing a book) Picture of Dorian Grey.*

MATT: Don't be so obsessed with youth.

PROFESSOR: *(Tossing a book) Moby Dick.*

MATT: Don't be so obsessed with the whale.

COACH: *Don Quixote.*

MATT: Sanity is overrated.

PROFESSOR: *(Tossing a book) One Flew Over the Cuckoo's Nest.*

MATT: Sanity is overrated.

COACH: *(Tossing a book) Harry Potter.*

MATT: Just overrated.

(Instead of stacking Harry Potter *on top of all the books in his arms, he throws it upstage over his shoulder.)*

PROFESSOR: *(Tossing a book) For Whom The Bell Tolls.*

MATT: Don't write long sentences.

COACH: *(Tossing* MATT *the* War and Peace Cliff Notes*) War and Peace.*

MATT: Don't write long books.

PROFESSOR: *Star Wars.*

MATT: Not a book, but Darth Vader is his father.

COACH: *Citizen Kane.*

MATT: Not a book, but Rosebud is his sled.

PROFESSOR: *(Tossing a book) Dianetics.*

MATT: Not a good book, but people will buy anything.

COACH: *(Tossing a book) Remembrance of Things Past.*

MATT: I like cookies.

PROFESSOR: *(Tossing a book) Tom Jones.*

MATT: What's new, pussycat?

COACH: *(Tossing a book) Beowulf.*

MATT: Don't make us read this crap.

PROFESSOR: *(Tossing a book) Lolita.*

MATT: Don't be such a pervert.

COACH: *(Tossing a book) The Fountainhead.*

MATT: Don't rely on anybody else.

PROFESSOR: *(Tossing a book) Death in Venice.*

MATT: I like that boy, but now I'm dead!

COACH: *(Tossing a book) Crime and Punishment.*

MATT: I killed that guy, but now I'm dead!

PROFESSOR: *(Tossing a book) Satanic Verses.*

MATT: I wrote that book, they want me dead!

COACH: *(Tossing a book) Bridges of Madison County.*

MATT: Don't write this crap!!

PROFESSOR: *(Tossing the last book) Gone With The Wind!*

MATT: Frankly, my dear—

ALL: —I don't give a damn!!! Finished!

(MATT places Gone With The Wind *atop the huge stack of books in his arms and throws the entire pile up into the air. The school bell rings. COACH, PROFESSOR and MATT high five each other. COACH and PROFESSOR point to MATT and applaud him. Finally the crowd quiets and COACH picks up the fake vampire teeth that fell out of MATT's mouth as DRACULA.)*

COACH: And we almost left out *White Fang* by Jack London. *(He casually tosses the teeth over his shoulder.)* Well, we didn't want to tell you this at the beginning because we knew you wouldn't do the work, but this has been a pass/fail course. Please distribute the diplomas. Congratulations, you all graduate!

(MATT and PROFESSOR each toss a stack of diplomas over the audience. Graduation music begins to play. Balloons fall from overhead.)

COACH: Thanks for coming. I'm... *(Actual name of actor).*

PROFESSOR: I'm... *(Actual name of actor).*

MATT: I'm... *(Actual name of actor)!*

ALL: And this was ALL THE GREAT BOOKS—
abridged! Good night!

(They bow, then high five and run up the aisle and out of the theater.)

EL FIN

PROFESSOR'S POEM
MEDLEY—ANNOTATED

For scholarly completists (you know who you are) here
are the poets and poems referenced by the PROFESSOR
in his Poem Medley.

There once was a man from Nantucket[1]
Whose string was so long he could pluck it[2]
He shot an arrow in the air
It fell to earth[3], there's no there there[4]
And in the depths of his despair cried, "Fie[5]
On the person who put me here
In the Ballad of Reading Gaol
Where each man kills the thing he loves
And loves the thing he nails.[6]"
Oh...Captain! My Captain![7]
We go down to the sea in ships[8]
The rhyming ancient mariner[9] stormed the beach
"Beware the Jabberwock, my son[10]
That dares to part his hair behind[11]
And in Xanadu did Kubla Khan[12] dare to eat a—
Peach[13], bananas, cucumbers...
Lettuce go, then, you and I
When evening is spread out amongst the sky[14]
Skylight burning bright[15]
First star I see tonight
Rage rage against the dying of the light
Do not go gentle into Gladys Knight[16]
Two roads diverged in a wood today[17]
How do I love thee? Let me count the way[18]

And I think that I shall never see a poem as lovely as
   Doris Day[19]
Into the valley of the dolls rode the six hundred[20]
On the eighteenth of April in seventy-five[21]
Seventy-six trombones led the big parade[22]
And I was stayin' alive, staying' alive[23]
O body swayed to music, O brightening glance
How can we know the dancer from the dance?[24]
I know why the caged bird sings the body electric[25]
And I'm a maniac
A maniac on the floor[26]
There is no joy in Mudville now that Casey knows the
   score[27]
Mighty Casey and
The Sunshine Band[28]
Quoth the raven, "Baltimore"[29]

[1] Perhaps the most famous line in the entire poem.
As far as we can discover, it was penned by the most
prolific writer who ever lived—Anonymous.

[2] We first heard this uttered by Edward Herrmann on
a classic episode of *Saint Elsewhere*, probably written by
Tom Fontana. As to its real authorship, a Google search
turns up two sites dedicated to Edna Saint Vincent
Millay and one dedicated to Nathaniel Hawthorne,
both of whom apparently loved to use the words
"string", "long", and "pluck", but never (as far as
we can tell) in the precise order used here. So what
the hell—let's say Edna Saint Vincent Millay.

[3] Here we go, the first genuine line of poetry written by
an identifiable person. In *The Arrow and the Song*, Henry
Wadsworth Longfellow wrote "I shot an arrow into the
air/It fell to earth, I knew not where..."

[4] Gertrude Stein coined this phrase. She was referring
(inaccurately, we can attest) to Oakland, California.

[5] Written by Austin to get to a word that started with the "F" sound, and which contained an internal "air" rhyme.

[6] Oscar Wilde wrote his famous poem "The Ballad of Reading Gaol" while incarcerated on obscenity charges. One stanza reads, "Yet each man kills the thing he loves,/By each let this be heard,/Some do it with a bitter look,/Some with a flattering word,/The coward does it with a kiss,/The brave man with a sword."

[7] Walt Whitman's *O Captain! My Captain!*, written upon hearing of the assassination of President Abraham Lincoln.

[8] The PROFESSOR knows this is a famous poetic phrase, but if he had a gun to his head he couldn't tell you that it's from the 107th Psalm ("They that go down to sea in ships, that do business in great waters: These see the works of the Lord, and his wonders in the deep").

[9] Samuel Taylor Coleridge wrote *The Rime of Ancient Mariner*. According to Merriam-Webster's Online Collegiate Dictionary, "rime" is "an accumulation of granular ice tufts on the windward sides of exposed objects that's formed from supercooled fog or cloud and built out directly against the wind." The PROFESSOR, of course, thinks "rime" means "words that sound alike."

[10] Lewis Carroll's famous poem *The Jabberwocky* is from his second Alice book, *Through The Looking Glass*.

[11] In *The Love Song of J Alfred Prufrock*, T S Eliot describes the timid title character as someone who "dares to part his hair behind".

[12] This is the opening line of Coleridge's poem *Kubla Khan*.

[13] This is T S Eliot again, describing Prufrock's questioning himself: "Do I dare to eat a peach?" (See note [11].)

[14] More Eliot, more *Prufrock*: this is a paraphrase of the opening two lines of *The Love Song of J Alfred Prufrock* ("Let us go then, you and I,/When the evening is spread out amongst the sky"). The PROFESSOR stumbles onto it because he picks up part of a grocery list and thinks "lettuce" is (are) the first word(s) of the poem.

[15] The PROFESSOR is now confusing William Blake's *The Tiger* ("Tiger! Tiger! burning bright") with nursery rhymes.

[16] Now he's confusing Dylan Thomas's *Do Not Go Gentle Into That Dark Night* with the lead singer of *Midnight Train To Georgia*. (Interestingly, for some reason, "rage rage against the dying of the light," from the same poem, is quoted exactly. This is almost certainly a mistake.)

[17] A paraphrase of the opening line of Robert Frost's poem *The Road Not Taken*: "Two roads diverged in a yellow wood."

[18] Another paraphrase, this time of Elizabeth Barrett Browning's "How Do I Love Thee?"

[19] The opening stanza of Joyce Kilmer's *Trees* ("I think that I shall never see a poem as lovely as a tree") is mistakenly used to invoke the majesty of kitschy fifties goddess Doris Day. Whether this reveals the PROFESSOR's desperation to rhyme, or accidentally outs his fondness for camp remains unclear.

[20] Those who believe the PROFESSOR's tendency towards camp rises dangerously close to the surface get more evidence here, when he unknowingly references Jacqueline Susann's camp classic *Valley of the Dolls* while attempting to quote Alfred, Lord Tennyson's *The*

Charge of the Light Brigade: ("Into the valley of Death/Rode the six hundred").

[21] This is the third line of the first stanza of Henry Wadsworth Longfellow's *Paul Revere's Ride*.

[22] Now hopelessly confused, the PROFESSOR is clinging to whatever bits of famous rhymes he can pull out of the air. This line, inspired by the last words of the previous line, is of course from Meredith Willson's *The Music Man*.

[23] The Professor relies on The Brothers Gibb (better known as The Bee Gees) to get him over this rhyming hump.

[24] A last-ditch attempt at an authentically scholarly poem, these are the last two lines of William Butler Yeats's appropriately titled *Among School Children*.

[25] In the home stretch now, PROFESSOR muddles Maya Angelou's classic volume of autobiography *I Know Why The Caged Bird Sings* with Walt Whitman's *Leaves of Grass*, although it's more likely the PROFESSOR knows "sing the body electric" as that song from the movie *Fame*.

[26] More evidence of the PROFESSOR's fabulously detailed knowledge of eighties movie musicals. Jennifer Beals danced famously to this song in *Flashdance*. It was written by Dennis Matkosky and Michael Sembello.

[27] This is of course from Ernest Lawrence Thayer's classic poem *Casey At The Bat*.

[28] The PROFESSOR has confused "Mighty Casey" the baseball player with mighty K C, he of the Sunshine Band. The Boogeyman.

[29] The haunting refrain of Edgar Allan Poe's *The Raven* is of course "Quoth the Raven, 'Nevermore'", but since Poe is actually from Baltimore, the PROFESSOR isn't completely wrong. In Europe, where knowledge of Poe,

Maryland cities, and the Baltimore Ravens football team isn't wide-spread, PROFESSOR said "Quoth the Raven, 'Elsinore'".

POETS / AUTHORS QUOTED
(in order of appearance)

Henry Wadsworth Longfellow
Gertrude Stein
Oscar Wilde
Walt Whitman
Samuel Taylor Coleridge
Lewis Carroll
T S Eliot
William Blake
Dylan Thomas
Robert Frost
Elizabeth Barrett Browning
Joyce Kilmer
Jacqueline Susann
Alfred, Lord Tennyson
Meredith Willson
The Bee Gees
William Butler Yeats
Maya Angelou
Dennis Matkosky and Michael Sembello
Ernest Lawrence Thayer
Edgar Allan Poe

THE SYLLABUS

The eighy-six books that this show claims to cover.
Actual Great Books may vary.

(This may be be used as a program insert.)

1984
The Aeneid
Alice in Wonderland
Animal Farm
Anna Karenina
Autobiography of Alice B. Toklas
Beowulf
Brave New World
Bridges of Madison County
The Brothers Karamazov
The Canterbury Tales
A Christmas Carol
The Count of Monte Cristo
Crime and Punishment
Das Capital
David Copperfield
Death in Venice
Dianetics
Diary of Anne Frank
The Divine Comedy
Don Quixote
Doctor Jekyll and Mister Hyde
Dracula
The Feminine Mystique
For Whom The Bell Tolls

The Fountainhead
Frankenstein
Gone With The Wind
The Grapes of Wrath
Great Expectations
The Great Gatsby
Green Eggs and Ham
Harry Potter & the Sorcerer's Stone
Heart of Darkness
Hound of the Baskervilles
Huckleberry Finn
Hunchback of Notre Dame
The Idiot
I Know Why The Caged Bird Sings
The Iliad
Interpretation of Dreams
The Invisible Man
Jaws
Leaves of Grass
Little Women
Lolita
Lord of the Flies
Metamorphosis
Middlemarch
Moby Dick
The Odyssey
Of Mice and Men
Oliver Twist
On The Road
One Flew Over The Cuckoo's Nest
The Origin of Species
Orlando
The Picture of Dorian Gray
Plato's Republic
Pride and Prejudice
Remembrance of Things Past
Samuel Johnson's Dictionary

The Satanic Verses
The Scarlet Letter
Sense and Sensibility
Silas Marner
Silent Spring
Sons and Lovers
The Story of Genji
A Tale of Two Cities
Tao Te Ching
TekWar
Tess of the D'Urbervilles
The Three Musketeers
Thus Spake Zarathustra
To Kill A Mockingbird
Tom Jones
To The Lighthouse
Treasure Island
Ulysses
Valley of the Dolls
Walden
War and Peace
White Fang
The Wizard of Oz
Wuthering Heights

On the following page is the Russian phrase for the sign that is referred to at the beginning of the *War and Peace* section on page 72:

Это - фактический русский. Вы впечатлены?